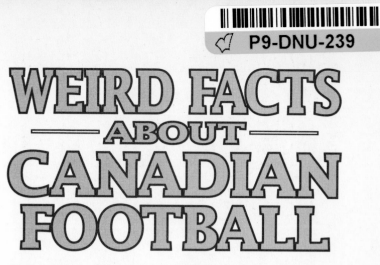

WEIRD FACTS ABOUT CANADIAN FOOTBALL

Strange, Wacky & Hilarious Stories

Stephen Drake

OVER TIME BOOKS

The Publisher: OverTime Books is an imprint of Éditions de la Montagne Verte

www.overtimebooks.com

Library and Archives Canada Cataloguing in Publication
Drake, Stephen, 1960–
   Weird facts about Canadian football : Strange, wacky & hilarious stories / Stephen Drake.

Includes bibliographical references.

ISBN 978-1-897277-26-3

   1. Canadian football—History—Miscellanea. 2. Canadian Football League—History—Miscellanea. I. Title.

GV948.D73 2008   796.33502   C2008-907472-6

Project Director: J. Alexander Poulton
Editor: Timothy Niedermann
Layout & Design: HR Media Group
Cover Image: Courtesy of iStockphoto.com; photographers: Taco Jim, Chris Hart

We acknowledge the financial support of the Government of Canada through the Book Publishing Industry Development Program (BPIDP) for our publishing activities.

 Canadian   Patrimoine
Heritage   canadien

PC: 5

Dedication

The deaths of Ron Lancaster, Earl Lunsford, Ralph Sazio, Don Wittman, Bob Ackles and Leif Pettersen in 2008—all them major figures in Canadian football—cast a sad pall over the season just completed. This book honours the legendary contributions they made to the game.

–Stephen Drake

Contents

Acknowledgements

For over 100 years, a devoted group of sports historians and journalists has documented the rich heritage and tradition of Canadian football. Their words have eloquently captured their passion for the game and helped make researching and writing this book a pleasure.

Introduction

Invariably Canadians are forced to compare their brand of football with the more glitzy and glamorous football of our neighbours to the south. The National Football League in the United States is big right now, really big. Supported by billions of dollars of television revenue, American football is pushed by a wave of marketing that spills over the border. Football fans in Canada are fed the NFL brand constantly, while our underdog Canadian Football League, with its undersized budget, scratches and claws for attention.

And indeed Canadian football is different. We play our game on a wider and longer field, with an extra player. The offence has one fewer down to gain 10 yards. But it is the very quirkiness of the CFL that makes it worth both cherishing and saving. For example, what other professional sports league, when it had only nine teams, would allow two of its franchises, the Saskatchewan Roughriders and the Ottawa Rough Riders, to have the same name? A short history lesson provides the answer: the Ottawa Rugby Club had used the handle "Rough Riders" since 1890, taking the moniker from the crazy lumberjacks who rode logs down the turbulent rapids of the Ottawa River, but the club switched its team name to the Senators in 1924. The Regina Roughriders were named after a pair of North West Mounted Police officers who had an equally perilous job in breaking the wild broncos used by the force. When Ottawa switched their name to the Senators, Regina officially snapped up the Roughriders tag. A few years later Ottawa reclaimed the Rough Riders name, which lived on in the nation's capital until the franchise folded in 1996.

Lumberjacks and bronco riders, how Canadian is that? And how about the Blue Bombers, the Eskimos and the Tiger-Cats? All of those names invoke a sense of Canadian tradition, and the century-old history of the CFL is littered with events that reflect the characteristics of our country: oversized and under-populated, having to make do with less.

This helps to explain how, in 1995, a pair of CFL teams selected a dead player in two separate drafts. The Ottawa Rough Riders took defensive end Derrell Robertson in a dispersal draft of Las

Vegas Posse players after the team folded. Ottawa coach Jim Gilstrap blamed part of the blunder on the list distributed by the CFL that showed Robertson as a potential draftee: "The league didn't know [of Robertson's death] until we told them," said Gilstap. "And we didn't know until we couldn't find him."

CFL chairman John Tory had a more cynical take on the matter: "I would think the first qualification they might want to come up with is that the person's alive."

A few months later, the Montréal Alouettes embarrassed themselves and the league at the college draft. The Alouettes drafted defensive end James Eggink from Northern Illinois. Eggink had died of cancer six months earlier.

NFL teams and the league itself employ an army of staff to make sure such embarrassments don't occur. CFL budgets are miniscule in comparison; stuff like that happens in Canada.

The CFL is a league where Winnipeg played for decades in the West Division and then moved to the East Division and then back to the West and then over to the East once again. In the 2008 season with the crossover playoff format, the Edmonton Eskimos played the Montréal Alouettes in the Eastern final. A break here or there and Calgary would have been playing Edmonton in the 2008 Grey Cup in Montréal. The timeless tradition of East versus West could have been thrown out the door, and one day it will be—the league dodged a bullet in 2008.

During the late 1980s and through the 1990s, the CFL was known as the Crazy Football League. The teams seemed to take turns with crooked, underfinanced, uninformed or plain senseless ownership. Almost every franchise was a phone call away from bankruptcy. The Ottawa Rough Riders folded. A team with over 100 years of history has now been on hiatus for over a decade, but optimism still prevails. A credible ownership group has been negotiating with the city of Ottawa to upgrade the stadium so football can return. The 2011 season is the target date.

Still, in the Canadian Football League there are always storms brewing. The most troubling are the inroads the NFL has made in Canada, or more accurately, Toronto. Over the next five years, the Buffalo Bills will play eight games in our largest city—five regular season tilts and three exhibitions. Rogers Communications leased the games from the Bills for $78 million. To re-coup that investment, NFL fans in Toronto are going to pay a lot of money for their tickets.

Some CFL supporters believe this is the first step in what could be the extinction of Canadian football. The feeling is that if the Bills moved to Toronto permanently, the Argos would eventually fold— corporate support would flow to the more high-profile American team, and, without the corporate support of Central Canada, the rest of the league would be in trouble. No one knows how this one will play out. Would football supporters in Toronto be willing to shell out $250 to watch a mediocre Buffalo team without any ties to the community when they could spend a tenth of that to watch the Boatmen play Hamilton—a game featuring Canadian players born and raised in Ontario?

Reginald Bibby, a sociologist from the University of Lethbridge, has written that it is "something of a cultural miracle" that the CFL has withstood the American media invasion. Bibby's conclusion sums up the continuing diligence that will be required to keep our quirky, yet exciting brand of football going in the future: "The CFL might be Canada's ugly duckling; but a remarkable duckling it is in an age when most things distinctively Canadian have gone the way of the U.S. cooking pot. Who knows what the CFL could look like if ethnocentric Americans could be persuaded to give it a closer look and masochistic Canadians stopped trying to put its head on the chopping block?"

Chapter One

The Grey Cup—Battered, Burned and Forgotten

The first Grey Cup game was played December 4, 1909, between the Toronto Parkdales and the University of Toronto. Almost 4000 fans watched as the varsity team prevailed 26–6. They were the first team to have their names inscribed on the $48 trophy that Governor General Albert Henry George Grey had donated to commemorate the Canadian football champion.

The only problem was that there was no trophy to present after the game ended. The trophy had been designed by Birks Jewellers in London, and it was supposed to have arrived from England in time for the championship, but weeks later it was still missing. Cup trustee H.B. McGiverin pointed out the urgency of receiving the trophy to A.F. Sladen of Government House in a rather short piece of correspondence:

My dear Sladen,

I am asked by the other two trustees what has become of the Grey Cup, so please let me know when we can expect it.

Four months later the Cup completed its trek to Canada, where it has remained for almost a century. Over that time, the trophy has suffered several bumps and bruises. The Cup's long history is only a partial explanation. In the beginning, because Canadian football lacked the popularity of other sports, the trophy was often hidden away in closets and back rooms during the off-season. In addition to neglect, the trophy has also taken a bit of a beating through the years. It seems the big, strong men who play football have a knack for breaking things, even the very trophy they've battled so hard to capture.

When the Hamilton Tiger-Cats won their second Grey Cup in 1915, the team commissioned a shield that was engraved with the Tiger-Cats as 1908 champions. And even though the trophy wasn't donated by Lord Grey until 1909, Hamilton went ahead and brazenly attached the shield to the original Grey Cup (and that shield is still attached to the Cup).

During World War I, the Grey Cup game was cancelled for three successive years, from 1916 through 1918, the trophy was left in a vault of a Toronto trust company. When it was rediscovered, one of the bank's trustees looked at the tarnished and dusty silver cup and said, "Get that thing out of here."

Even after the war, the Cup was still treated with disregard. Hamilton manager Len Back left the trophy in a closet for a year after the Tiger-Cats won it in 1928. Almost 20 years later the trophy survived a close call. In 1947, fire gutted the Toronto Argonaut Rowing Cup clubhouse where it was stored. All of the other trophies had fallen from their shelves and been melted by the fire, but the Grey Cup had gotten snagged on a large nail and never reached the floor. Although blackened, with its base badly charred, the Cup survived.

The Grey Cup is symbolic of more than just a football game. It has become a festival, a celebration of Canadian sport. Between 3.5 and 4 million of us watch the championship game every year. It may have taken a beating over its long history, but Lord Grey's $48 trophy survives—its symbolism ever evolving as our young country continues to come of age.

Held for Ransom

In 1969, the Grey Cup survived its most bizarre mishap. On December 20, the trophy was stolen from a display case in Lansdowne Park in Ottawa. No other trophies were taken. A ransom letter demanded a large sum of money, but the CFL refused to pay.

An Ottawa police inspector named Hobbs was assigned to the case and informed the league that he saw the incident as a prank. Inspector Hobbs was sure that the Cup would show up if everyone was patient. When CFL Commissioner Jake Gaudaur suggested a reward, the police advised waiting until Christmas.

The story had faded from the news when, on January 4, 1970, both the Ottawa police and Ottawa Roughriders general manager Frank Clair received several phone messages. The caller said he knew where the trophy was and was willing to act as a go-between for a reward of between $100 and $500. The next day, the caller met with Inspector Hobbs and told him the price was $100 and four Ottawa season tickets.

Commissioner Gaudaur was sceptical that their intermediary had any real knowledge of the Cup's whereabouts: "A statement by the informer that at the moment the trophy was filled with biscuits in the possession of the thief, led me to wonder whether or not the informer was as full of biscuits as the trophy."

More time passed, and, with no news of the trophy's fate, the league decided to manufacture a replica. The original, if it was ever found, would be permanently housed in the Hall of Fame. Gaudaur joked about who some of the prime suspects might be: "The last four people seen with the trophy, photographically speaking, were Prime Minister Trudeau, myself, Russ Jackson and Ken Lehman. I just throw that out for what it is worth."

On February 16, 1970, Greg Fulton, the league's secretary-treasurer, received a call from the Toronto police. The police department had received a call to proceed to a phone booth at the corner of Parliament and Dundas streets. The police were instructed to look in the coin-return box for a key that would fit into a locker at the Royal York Hotel. When the locker was opened, the unharmed Grey Cup was waiting.

The Toronto police also had some fun when they placed a sticker on the trophy on the spot reserved for the 1970 winner. It read: "Metro Police ETF" [Emergency Task Force]. In 1972 the league approved a silver-plated replica of the Cup. The cost: $550, plus provincial sales tax.

The original trophy is permanently displayed at the CFL Hall of Fame.

In 1983, there was another Cup-napping scare. This one had less of a criminal overtone. A fraternity at the University of BC threatened to take the trophy and hold it for ransom so the money could be donated to charity. The prank never materialized.

Where Did I Leave It...?

Although the Regina Roughriders made six straight trips to the Grey Cup between 1928 and 1934, it was the Winnipeg 'Pegs who became the first Western team to claim the championship, in 1935. But the trip to Hamilton bankrupted the 'Pegs, and a club executive from Winnipeg, Les Isard, ended up having to pay the hotel bill. As the team boarded the train to head home, a quick search revealed the trophy had gone missing. No one could find it. "It's probably down in Sarnia," commented Winnipeg manager Joe Ryan. "We don't care very much if we ever get it, but I suppose it'll come along later."

In 1964, the BC Lions won their first championship. For the preceding 10 years, the Lions' management had spent nearly a million dollars to build their expansion team from scratch. A wild party at the Park Plaza Hotel in Toronto ensued after their victory. When the team checked out of the hotel the next day, they left the Cup behind. Just before the team boarded the flight home to Vancouver, someone finally noticed that the trophy was missing. A staff member returned to the hotel, where the Cup was located and for the first time made the trip to the West Coast.

In 1983, Toronto player Jan Carinci was bringing the trophy to a post-game celebration event. The Argos were saluting another Grey Cup win, and Carinci was given the job of escorting the championship silverware. On the way to the party, his car broke down on the highway. Carinci took the bag holding the trophy out of the trunk and began hitchhiking. A short time later a driver stopped to offer a ride. The only problem was that he was going in the other direction. The would-be chauffeur noticed the bag Carinci was carrying.

"What's in the bag?" he asked.

"The Grey Cup," replied Carinci.

"C'mon," said the driver sceptically.

Carinci took the Cup out of the bag. The driver was so impressed that he changed directions and took the Argo receiver directly to the restaurant.

A year later, Winnipeg general manager Paul Robson was the last member of the team to leave a civic reception at Winnipeg Arena a few days after the Blue Bombers had won the championship game. After he had left the building, Robson realized he had left the Cup behind. He rushed back to the arena to find the trophy still sitting at centre stage in the almost empty arena: "There it was, sitting up on the stage all by itself, and there were still people in the building. The funny thing is that this is what it's all about, and here we are forgetting it. Whoops!"

Pounding on the Cup

The players themselves have also directed some licks at the championship trophy. And even Grey Cup alumni have had mishaps with Lord Grey's trophy. In the late 1960s, Don Smith, co-chair of a Blue Bomber alumni dinner, was granted permission to bring the Cup to Winnipeg for the event. Smith, a fullback with the team in the 1940s, and some of the organizers were sharing stories in the hospitality suite of a downtown hotel into the wee hours of the morning. After deciding it was time to end the festivities, they walked through an alley on the way to their own hotel. The Cup fell apart in Smith's hands.

The base went rolling one way, the Cup the other. "Here we were down on our hands and knees looking for pieces, and a policeman walked by and asked us what we were doing," explained Smith. "We told him we were looking for pieces of the Grey Cup, but I don't think he believed us at first. He helped us look for a while. Fortunately, nothing was damaged."

In 1978, Edmonton captains Dan Kepley and Tom Wilkinson had accepted the Cup and were parading it around the field in Toronto after the Eskimos had avenged a loss to Montréal in the previous year's championship game. "There were a lot of people on the field, and some guy falls in front of us down by the goalposts," recalled Wilkinson. "He fell right in front of me, and I let go figuring 'OK, Kep's got it,' but he'd stopped to help the guy. I'm sure he knew I was the weightlifter, so he figured I had it."

The Cup fell to the hard turf. Once again the cup portion and the base separated. "I caught a lot of flak for that one," said Wilkinson. "They were on my back until the next year when we won again. This time it didn't drop and break."

In 1985, BC centre Al Wilson was made custodian of the Cup after the Lions had beaten the Tiger-Cats in Montréal. After attending the winning team festivities, Wilson and his wife, Robin, took some friends to see the sights. And of course they took the Grey Cup. "I took it on a tour of Montreal," said Wilson later. "I took it to all the strip joints and cabarets. We did Montréal until four in the morning. I wasn't trying to show it off or anything, but nobody could believe somebody was in downtown Montréal with the Grey Cup at two in the morning. Everybody just wanted to see it. I let people look at it, but I didn't let go of it."

After the Edmonton Eskimos' 1987 Grey Cup win, the trophy was sat on during the post-game celebration and broke again. Five years later, in 1993, Blake Dermott decided to start a new tradition by head-butting the Cup. He cracked the trophy at the neck.

In 2006, the BC Lions captured the Cup with a 25–14 win over the Montréal Alouettes in Winnipeg. During the on-field celebration after the game ended, the trophy broke when the cup portion fell off the base, which contains the engraved names of the players, coaches, executives and staff on each years' winning team. Lions' offensive guard Kelly Bates was holding the Grey Cup above his head when it snapped in two.

The Cup turning into two pieces didn't faze the Lions—the players simply hoisted both parts as they celebrated. "I have a feeling it was broken a few times in the past," laughed Bates afterwards.

Grey Cup ambassadors Mario Vespa and Paul Micieli, who had the job of looking after the famous trophy, were shocked when it came apart. "At one point I had looked up and there was a stream of confetti, and the only thing I could see was the top of the Cup," recalled Micieli of the Cup celebration on the field. "Once the confetti cleared, I noticed that all I could see was the top of the Cup. The base was on the other side."

The next day, Vespa and Micieli took the two pieces to Quest Metal Products in Winnipeg for emergency repairs. Ben Klumper, a veteran welder, was given the assignment of putting it back together.

"I wasn't sitting down at the time but I probably should have, because my hands started shaking and trembling," said Klumper in an interview with CBC television. "This isn't just some restaurateur coming with a broken fork or a broken pot that I got to fix. No this is the Grey Cup. So was I nervous? Absolutely."

As everyone in the shop stood around to watch the welder with 45 years of know-how reattach the base to the cup, Klumper said the job was one of the highlights of his career: "This was a once-in-a-lifetime experience. It wasn't just a job to weld this back together—it was an honour."

Klumper also got to keep a souvenir of his work—a piece of 100-year-old metal that had come off the trophy.

By the end of the day, the Cup was back with the Lions before they flew home to Vancouver. As 100 fans watched the team disembark from the plane, it was receiver Geroy Simon, not Kelly Bates, who was hoisting the repaired trophy.

"It's better now," said Bates at the airport. "I made the Cup better if you ask me. I thought it would be a lot more solid. It obviously wasn't, and now they've fixed it, so it won't do that again. I also broke the junior championship trophy when I played with the Saskatoon Hilltops. And I'm not that strong."

Grey Cup Bloopers and Trivia

After winning the first Grey Cup in 1909, the University of Toronto didn't want to give the trophy up, even though they didn't even qualify for the final game again until 1912. The university believed they should get to hold on to it until another team beat them in the championship.

In 1912, 6000 fans eagerly awaited the Grey Cup game between the Hamilton Alerts and the Toronto Argonauts. The only problem was they couldn't find the football. An hour later someone remembered that it was locked in the dressing room at the nearby Hamilton Cricket Grounds. When the person with the key couldn't be found, the door was kicked in, the ball retrieved and the game started. It cost $1.75 to fix the door.

Three years later, the Hamilton Tigers defeated the Toronto Rowing and Athletic Association 13–7 in the Grey Cup final. The game was marred by several controversial decisions by referee Ewart "Reddy" Dixon. The spectators and Dixon began exchanging insults, and, after the final whistle, dozens of fans poured onto the field to go after him. While police armed with batons tried to disperse the mob, Dixon ran for safety. The only available sanctuary, however, was the Toronto dressing room. The losing players had to endure not only the disappointment of the outcome, but the presence of the referee who had overseen their defeat and then more insults as Dixon continued his tirade in a safer but still less than sympathetic environment.

The 1920s saw the first Western challenge for the Grey Cup (in 1921 the Edmonton Eskimos lost 23–0 to Toronto) and the last university team to win the trophy (the Queens University Golden Gaels in 1924). In 1936, universities officially withdrew from Grey Cup competition.

In 1926, the Grey Cup game was played in the frigid cold of Toronto's Varsity Stadium. The field had turned into a sheet of ice; the football was rock-hard. The December 4 contest was played in such poor conditions that a small riot broke out before game time. People stormed the ticket booth demanding a refund. The angry spectators were turned away, and the Toronto officials closed the box office.

Three years later, in the title game between the Hamilton Tigers and the Regina Roughriders, the referee was doing his best to stay with the play as it neared the Regina goal line. Running at full speed, the official ran straight in to the goal post and was knocked out cold. Despite suffering the effects of a concussion, however, the referee returned to finish the game.

In the 1931 Grey Cup, the Montréal Winged Wheelers defeated Regina, but the game was best remembered for a change in footwear that Montréal made at halftime. In the second half, the Winged Wheelers dominated Regina.

Roughriders coach Al Ritchie blamed himself for not getting the right footwear to his team. Little did he know that the shoes Ritchie had ordered were actually delivered to the Montréal dressing room by mistake.

In 1939, the Grey Cup was played on December 9. For the week leading up to the big game, the weather fluctuated between rain and cold. The day before the contest, the temperature plunged, and the field turned rock-hard. In an attempt to soften things up, the grounds crew poured 400 gallons of gasoline on the field and set it ablaze. Freezing temperatures the eve of the game wiped out the benefits of the fire, and the field hardened again. To make matters worse, there was heavy snow at game time. Winnipeg edged the Ottawa Rough Riders 8–7.

With the start of World War II in 1939, the CFL faced a major challenge in keeping itself afloat. Players from all teams enlisted in the military, leaving the league's rosters depleted. The Western teams were especially decimated; with smaller populations they could barely recruit enough players to keep operating. In consequence, CFL league play was suspended after the 1941 Grey Cup until the war ended.

The military decided to step in. Realizing how valuable the game was to the morale of

Canadians, the military decided to organize football across the country. Military bases formed teams by recruiting CFL players who had enlisted. Non-civilian squads won the Grey Cup for the next three years. When the Toronto RCAF Hurricanes defeated the Winnipeg RCAF Bombers 8–5 in the 1942 Grey Cup, the game was broadcast to Canadian forces based in England. Military competition for the Grey Cup ended in 1945.

The first televised Grey Cup game was in 1952. The Toronto Argonauts and the Edmonton Eskimos faced each other—it was estimated that 700,000 people in the Toronto area alone watched the game. During the third quarter, the microwave receiver failed. It took crews 29 minutes to get the game back on the air, but fans were still able to watch the exciting conclusion as the Argos defeated the Eskimos 21–11.

Three years later, the Grey Cup game moved west of Ontario for the first time. The newly completed Empire Stadium in Vancouver was the enticement, and the CFL expected record gate revenue from the game. The host city didn't disappoint as a Cup-best 39,417 fans jammed into the stadium. Gate receipts totalled almost $200,000, another Grey Cup record.

In 1961, overtime was needed for the first time to decide a Grey Cup winner. In one of the hardest hitting championship games, Winnipeg and Hamilton renewed their bitter rivalry. The Tiger-Cats led 14–4 in the third quarter, but the Blue Bombers tied the score with six minutes remaining on a Ken Ploen touchdown run.

Overtime consisted of two 10-minute halves. Both teams were scoreless in the first session. Three minutes into the second overtime, Ploen evaded three Hamilton defenders to score an 18-yard game-winning touchdown, as Winnipeg prevailed 21–14.

The second overtime session in Cup history came in the 2005 classic at BC Place Stadium. Two other traditional rivals, Edmonton and Montréal faced off in one of the most exciting games in Grey Cup lore. Alouettes kicker Damon Duval forced the overtime when he kicked a 27-yard field goal with no time remaining on the clock.

Both teams traded touchdowns in the first overtime session. Early in the second overtime, Eskimos kicker Sean Fleming booted a 36-yard field goal to give Edmonton the lead. The Alouettes had one final opportunity to tie the game again, but a penalty and a sack of Montréal quarterback Anthony Calvillo pushed the ball out of field goal range. In desperation, Calvillo tried punting on third down hoping an Alouette would recover the kick, but Edmonton held on to the ball to seal 38–35 victory.

Chapter Two

The Cursed Weather

Snow, rain, wind and cold—the unpredictability of Canadian football is due in part to the nasty weather of late autumn. Despite the addition of indoor stadiums in Toronto and Vancouver, football in Canada is still best enjoyed as an outdoor sport. At its most compelling, football is framed by the frosted breath of opposing linemen, their bare arms exposed as they prepare to charge into each other on the frozen turf of a prairie field. Football is most challenging when a quarterback delivers an accurate pass with a rain-soaked ball, when a cornerback cuts in perfect synchrony with the receiver he is covering on a muddy field or when a running back stays on his feet despite the perils of icy turf as defenders slip and slide around him.

For almost 100 years, teams have battled to win the Grey Cup trophy in late November and early December. The game has become part of the Canadian tradition. That long heritage has included a series of championship games made memorable by the conditions on the field.

The Mud Bowl

On the eve of the 1950 Grey Cup in Toronto, eight inches of snow fell on the city. A snow-removal truck was brought in to clear the field, but the snow turned to rain and the truck became stuck in the mud. A tractor truck had to be brought in to tow it out, leaving huge ruts on the playing surface in the process. The unprotected field was left a mess.

The Canadian Rugby Union, which ran the CFL in those days, had been criticized the year before for not investing $6000 to buy a tarpaulin for just such situations. As Scott Young, a sports columnist with the Toronto *Globe and Mail* wrote at the time: "Every time I heard a car backfire Saturday night...I thought someone had shot a CRU official."

As the Toronto Argonaut and Winnipeg Blue Bomber players slid around in the goop, little did the 27,000 fans who showed up at Varsity Stadium realize a that life-and-death situation may have been unfolding before them. Early in the game, referee Hec Creighton of Toronto saw a Winnipeg player lying face down in ankle deep slush. Luckily Creighton recognized that something was amiss and managed to turn the player, 268-pound lineman Buddy Tinsley, on his back.

Over the years the near-drowning incident grew to mythical proportions. Tinsley downplayed the seriousness of the situation. "I wasn't drowning," he insisted. "But the weather was atrocious that day. There was water floating on the field and pieces of ice. I had hurt my knee in the playoffs. They taped my knee and my quadriceps so tight that the muscles wouldn't move. I happened to get hit right on the thigh real hard. That paralyzed my leg, and I fell forward. I was lying there with my head on my arm very unhappy because I had got hurt. I was just laying there because I couldn't move my leg. A couple of guys came over and helped me up. I don't know how that story got started. I think people in the stands thought I was drowning because of the conditions."

The Argonauts ended up negotiating the slop more effectively and defeated Winnipeg 13–0. The Blue Bombers, led by quarterback Jack Jacobs were normally a superb passing team, but were unable to adjust to the slippery conditions. Toronto quarterback Al Dekdebrun didn't have the same problem moving the ball through the air. Afterwards Dekdebrun revealed his secret to reporters. Before the game he had the trainer tape thumbtacks to his fingers with just enough of the points sticking out to grip the ball.

The Fog Bowl

The weather turned so ugly at the 1962 Grey Cup that the game had to be played over two days. An unseasonable warm spell caused a dense fog to roll into Toronto off of Lake Ontario, slowly encasing CNE Stadium as the game progressed. Although the players and coaches at field level could see what was going on, the crowd in the stands and the television audience were left guessing at what action was taking place below them.

At one point CBC broadcaster Johnny Esaw attested to the limitations of his play-by-play call to the folks watching the game at home, admitting, "I really don't know what's going on down there." And the late, legendary ABC sportscaster Jim McKay, who was calling the game for an American TV audience, raved about the entertainment value of the battle between Winnipeg and Hamilton: "This is the greatest football spectacle of them all. I've not seen hitting as hard as this in any game…what a pity the fog had to spoil it."

By the third quarter, the paying customers were losing their patience. One full-throated fan high up in the stands yelled: "Only one thing left to do. Let's get down to some serious drinking." When a fight erupted between a Winnipeg fan and a Hamilton supporter over some spilt popcorn, a full-scale brawl threatened to break out. The police arrived in time to cool things down, much to the dismay of a Westerner who had made the trip.

"Well," yelled the disgruntled spectator, "how d'ya like that. It costs me five hundred bucks to come here this week, and they break up the only action I can see."

As the fog continued to thicken, CFL commissioner G. Sydney Halter had a difficult to decision to make. Winnipeg wanted the game to continue (they were ahead by a point), while, not surprisingly, Hamilton wanted a new game to be scheduled the next week. After consulting with the weather office, Halter suspended the contest with less than 10 minutes remaining in the fourth quarter and ordered that it resume again the following day.

At a press conference Halter declared: "If play is started Sunday it will be finished regardless of the weather. But if it is impossible to start, I intend to recommend that the game remain unfinished and be declared no contest."

Both coaches had 22 hours to strategize for the next day. The Blue Bombers were in a bit of a quandary. Traditionally the Saturday night after the Grey Cup was a time for the players to let loose, but nursing just a one-point lead made the final outcome anything but certain. Winnipeg coach Bud Grant left it to the players to decide on a curfew time and everyone complied.

Both teams had another challenge as they suited up the next day. Football players need time to heal after throwing themselves at each other for 60 minutes. The locker rooms were like emergency wards. Blue Bomber legend Frank Rigney recalled how bad things were on the Winnipeg side, "It was a scary locker room. Guys were screaming in pain as they were getting shot up with painkillers."

When the sore and tired teams resumed the battle on a clear Sunday afternoon, only 15,000 of the original 32,655 fans returned to the stadium. Over the final 10 minutes, the score remained unchanged as Winnipeg held on for a 28–27 victory.

After the game, Commissioner Halter was criticized for allowing the Grey Cup to go as scheduled on the Saturday, even though the fog had been forecast. Halter denied that ABC had pressured the CFL to keep the same schedule, even though the league was eager to showcase the Grey Cup on the *Wide World of Sports* to an American audience of about 22 million. In the end, a tight contest between two evenly matched teams was overshadowed by the elements.

The Wind Bowl

Instead of fog or mud, Toronto added gale-force winds to the mix in the 1965 Grey Cup between Winnipeg and Hamilton. Westerly gusts between 55 and 80 kilometres per hour whipped off Lake Ontario and into CNE Stadium. The resulting conditions resulted in the officials changing the rules and in the Winnipeg coach making a questionable strategic decision.

The referees would forego calling the five-yard "no yards" rule (which gives the punt returner a five-yard buffer zone when fielding a kick); instead, when the punter was kicking into the wind, the play would be called dead once the ball contacted the returner. The windy conditions caused 50 of the 60 minutes to be played in the east end of the stadium.

On one play in the third quarter, Blue Bomber punter Ed Ulmer kicked from the Winnipeg 25-yard line. The punt boomed off Ulmer's foot, and then, as if in slow motion, it virtually stopped in mid-air and came back to him. Hamilton linebacker John Barrow happened to be standing right where the ball landed, took it before Ulmer could jump on it and ran in for a touchdown. The officials, however, ruled that the ball was dead where it hit the turf.

On another punt attempt on the Hamilton side, Tiger-Cat kicker Joe Zuger chased after his own short kick and ran right into Winnipeg returner Dick Worney. Another Hamilton player jumped on the loose ball, but the rule change meant that the Blue Bombers kept possession. Two plays later, Winnipeg scored a touchdown.

No one was certain what the officials would decide with each punt. And no one bothered to tell the fans that the rules had been changed due to the wind. Legendary Winnipeg coach Bud Grant added to the confusion when he decided it was too risky to attempt kicks deep in his own end. Instead, on three separate possessions he ordered his punter to run back into his own end zone and concede a two-point safety. In giving up the points, Grant reasoned that his team would get to keep the ball, denying the Tiger-Cats the opportunity to score touchdowns on short drives deep in the Winnipeg end of the field.

Grant's logic was sound, but sports reporters and fans later heaped plenty of criticism on his decision. Hamilton won the classic 22–16; the three conceded safeties ended up as the margin of difference.

Even after the contest, Grant never wavered in defending his strategy: "We really didn't have any choice. We thought it was better to give up six points than a possible 21. Under the same circumstances, we'd have done the same thing again." It was Grant's last appearance in the Grey Cup before heading south to coach in the NFL.

God Intervenes

In 1969, the Toronto Argonauts had enjoyed a stellar 10–4 season and were favoured to represent the East in the Grey Cup. But first they had to get by the Ottawa Rough Riders in a two-game total-point playoff to advance to the Cup. The Rough Riders handed the Argos three of their four losses during the regular season, but Toronto beat their eastern rivals 22–14 in the first playoff game.

The long-suffering Argonaut fans hadn't seen their team in the Grey Cup since 1952. For the 10 years between 1956 and 1966, they had only averaged four wins a season. But, led by the always-quotable Toronto coach Leo Cahill, the Argos had become a league power. Cahill charmed the fans and press with his Irish wit, but with effective recruiting and some deft trading, he also rebuilt the ailing franchise.

Two days after the first victory over Ottawa, at a luncheon in Toronto, Cahill confidently stated, "It will take an act of God to beat us," and then followed up another bold statement that the Argos were "physically better than any team in Canada." The press played up the coach's quotes, setting the stage for a grudge-filled match the following week in Ottawa.

The night before Saturday's game, heavy rain combined with a sudden cold snap turned Ottawa's Lansdowne Park into a skating rink. The Ottawa trainers outfitted the Rough Rider players with broomball shoes, while the Argos flopped around in conventional cleats. Led by the brilliant quarterbacking of Russ Jackson, Ottawa totally dominated in a 32–3 romp, winning the two-game series 46–25.

The Riders, their fans and the press weren't shy in throwing Cahill's divinely inspired words back at him. Some said Jackson didn't need a ride to Lansdowne Park that afternoon; he just walked across the ice floes of the Rideau Canal to get to the game. Others said that even if the Twelve Apostles had suited up for the Argos, the outcome would have been the same.

Cahill took it all in stride and said his comments had been taken out of context. "I'm a Midwest kid from Illinois," he explained. "One of the things they have in the farm country is the act of God thing. If the crops get ruined by a storm or frost or anything else, it is called an act of God. I was referring to the weather. What happened was we went over there, and it was icy. They wore broomball shoes and we didn't, and they beat the hell out of us."

It would take the Argos another two years to finally reward their fans with a trip to the 1971 Grey Cup against Calgary, where fate cruelly intervened again to deny the Boatmen a championship.

The Argo Bounce

It was a can't-miss year for the Toronto Argo-nauts, who rolled to a 10–4 season and then dis-patched Hamilton to advance to the 1971 Grey Cup. It was Toronto's first trip to the champion-ship game since 1952. Their opponents were the Calgary Stampeders, who hadn't won the classic since 1948.

Vancouver was the host city, so there wasn't too much concern about snow, ice, wind or even fog. Even rain wasn't an issue, not with the arti-ficial turf at Empire Stadium—the Lions venue was the only CFL stadium in the country where mud was not a factor.

The conditions favoured the Argos and their high-powered offence led by Joe Theismann, a Heismann Trophy winner, at quarterback, two talented running backs in Bill Symons and rookie Leon McQuay, and a receiving corps that included all-stars Bobby Taylor and Mel Profit.

The all-weather field was put to the test all week—a West Coast Special settled in, and it rained and rained and rained some more. The drainage system couldn't handle the deluge, and the turf began to collect the water. For good mea-sure it rained all through the game, making the slick synthetic field even more slippery.

The conditions seemed to favour the upstart Stampeders who held a 14–3 lead at halftime. The Argos closed the gap in the second half, first on a fumble off a Calgary punt and then a single point off a missed field goal. With a little more than two minutes to play, Stampeders quarterback Jerry Keeling tried a deep pass to put the Argos away. Instead, it was intercepted and returned to the Calgary 11-yard line.

A field goal would now tie the game, and a touchdown would give the Argos victory. After picking up three yards on first down, Toronto elected to keep the ball on the ground—at the very least it would be an easy field goal attempt. Then came the "Argo Bounce."

Over the years, no one has really agreed on what this means. Good luck, bad luck, a curse, a jinx or a run of good fortune. It stands simply as a metaphor for everything that has befallen the Toronto franchise, good and bad—injuries, trades, hirings and firings—but when it doesn't work out, fans blame the Argo Bounce.

On that rainy afternoon in Vancouver, quarterback Theismann handed the ball to running back McQuay on second down. McQuay's job was to go down when he was in the middle of the field, giving the kicker an easy angle for the field goal attempt. But McQuay, who had a brilliant 1000-yard rushing season, saw an opening, the opportunity to win the game with a touchdown run.

Did the rookie factor in the rain, the wet ball and the slippery field? The fleet-footed back made his cut and down he went in a puddle of water. The ball came loose, and a Calgary defender jumped on it. Despite some nervous moments in the time remaining, the Stampeders held on to win the Cup.

After the game, McQuay relived the mishap for the press: "Hell, it was an end sweep left and I was closed off wide so I tried to cut and I slipped and my right elbow hit the ground and it just popped up. It was real wet, and it just popped up."

Leo Cahill, the popular Argos coach later commented: "When Leon McQuay slipped, I fell"— a reference to his dismissal a few days later. It was a nasty case of the Argo Bounce.

The Cold...Real Cold

Football players don't like to complain about the weather. After all, the sport is played outdoors in all kinds of conditions by huge, tough men who run over each other for 60 minutes.

But fans who show up for the game have the right to fume: they have to sit on hard molded-plastic chairs or unforgiving wood bleachers. And the quality of the contest is often diminished by those same conditions—skill is replaced by brute strength and good fortune.

The 1975 Grey Cup in Calgary was one of those games. Edmonton and Montréal battled on the frozen turf in McMahon Stadium. Earlier in the week, the weather had been balmy, and the Calgarians had hosted the Grey Cup festivities without needing coats. On Friday, a cold front settled in. Saturday was worse, and on game day the temperature dipped to –10°C. Add the wind chill and it was at least –30°C, the most frigid Grey Cup in history.

Edmonton quarterback Bruce Lemmerman recalled the severity of the cold: "After we'd been out there about five minutes trying to warm up, I turned to one of the guys and said we might as well go in, this was a waste of time. The temperature was down to minus 25 degrees. There was no way we were going to get warm. I remember the big long tubes along the side-lines with the hot air blowing in. The players were sitting on them. You hated to get up and go on the field. I carried a charcoal hand-warmer the entire game."

As might be expected, the game was a defensive struggle. For only the third Grey Cup there were no touchdowns—all the scoring in Edmonton's 9–8 victory came from the kicking of the Eskimos' Dave Cutler and the Alouettes' Don Sweet. Montréal had a golden opportunity to win the game on a last-second field goal attempt, but the holder's frozen hands caused him to misplay the snap.

For Eskimos great middle linebacker Dan Kepley, an American, it was his first Grey Cup: "I had no idea what a Grey Cup was. But I knew I had to win that game just to pay for the down-filled jackets and clothes I had to buy my Dad and his best friend when they came up for the game."

The Staple Bowl

In 1977, Edmonton and Montréal again met in the Grey Cup. This time, the Alouettes had the advantage of hosting the classic at Olympic Stadium. And once again, the weather was a major contributor to the game's storyline.

The day before the game, Montréal was hit by a major snowstorm. Olympic Stadium had an exposed field in those days and, despite the billion-dollar cost of the Big O, had no tarp to cover the playing surface. The grounds crew scrambled to remove the snow but left behind a wet field that froze overnight when the temperature plunged. The next day, workmen spread salt pellets on the field to melt the ice, but doing that left a slimy chemical sheen on the artificial turf, which made it even more treacherous.

At kickoff time, the temperature was −9°C, and the field was a mess. A record crowd of 68,205 watched what should have been a close contest between two excellent teams turn into an error-plagued affair that, fortunately for the hometown fans, ended up going Montréal's way in a 41–6 romp.

Edmonton repeatedly turned the ball over, while Montréal quarterback Sonny Wade seemed to handle the slippery conditions with ease, gingerly avoiding the Eskimos' pass rush before zipping the ball to a wide-open receiver. The Alouettes had crafted a significant advantage— defensive back Tony Proudfoot had the idea of putting heavy-duty staples into the shoes of the Montréal players.

"Tony Proudfoot had the idea," confirmed Montreal defensive star Gene Gaines. "He said this is really effective. So he popped some staples into his shoes, and then some other guys grabbed a staple gun and went boom, boom, boom. We found out during the first half that they were effective. At halftime everyone else had them in their shoes."

When the staples-in-the-shoes caper was discovered after the game, several Eskimos complained that Montréal had had an unfair advantage. Alouette defensive star Wally Buono, who later went on to a successful CFL coaching career, disagreed: "We didn't win because of the staples—we won because we were a better football team. We had beaten the Eskimos in Edmonton that year. We had a closely-knit group of guys who really played hard and intensely. That's why we won."

The Tundra Bowl

The 1984 Grey Cup was another cold game, this one in Edmonton, as 60,081 fans jammed into Commonwealth Stadium in 1984 to watch Winnipeg pummel Hamilton 47–17. The temperature during the national anthem was –11°C and dropped to –17°C by the final play.

The Hamilton defenders were slipping and sliding all afternoon trying to chase down the Blue Bomber receivers. Ticat kicker Bernie Ruoff had a terrible time trying to stay on his feet. On the Winnipeg side, though, the receivers and defensive backs seemed to have little trouble with the conditions. Again it came down to a shoe adjustment. Blue Bomber equipment man Len Amey had outfitted many of his players with baseball shoes recommended by the Toronto Blue Jays. It was a plastic-based shoe with a baseball cleat on the outside and smaller spikes on the interior of the sole. This helped cut through the thin layer of ice that had formed on the frozen turf, improving traction enormously, and made the final result almost a foregone conclusion.

Chapter Three

With Great Power Comes Great Irresponsibility

Jim Coleman, the great Canadian sports journalist, sarcastically summed up the contributions made by the CFL's owners over the years: "Canadian football must be a great game, because it survives in spite of the men who run it."

Coleman's famous quote came years before the stable of wacky owners the league went through in the 1980s and 1990s. Up to that time, many CFL teams were controlled by the community (BC, Edmonton, Calgary, Saskatchewan and Winnipeg) and run by a board of directors. There were plenty of backroom battles in the boardroom, but for the most part, there was consistency on the field and a sense of ongoing survival.

When the league hit tough economic times in the late 1980s, the passion of dedicated volunteer board members started to fade. Private owners stepped in with cash to keep teams afloat. It was a time when the off-field antics of new owners often gained more media attention than what was happening on the gridiron.

Harold Ballard

Over the many years that he owned the Toronto Maple Leafs and the Hamilton Tiger-Cats, Harold Ballard was described as profane, a bully, a boor, loyal, sentimental, generous and charitable. Whether he was admired or despised, most people that came into contact with him agreed he was larger than life.

Ballard was always in the news. He provided colourful quotes to the media on various topics—feminism, gay rights and foreign governments, to name a few. He publicly criticized his employees, managers, coaches and players alike. He ran a public company like it was his personal fiefdom and went to jail as a result. He even fought his own family in open court.

"Harold is a nice guy," remarked Jim Coleman once. "It's just that sometimes when he wakes up in the morning he forgets to do up the zipper in his head."

By the time he died in 1990, Ballard had become a caricature of the bombastic, eccentric and ego-driven sports owner. But unlike his contemporaries in other sports, such as George Steinbrenner (baseball) and Al Davis (NFL football), who each won several championships, Ballard for the most part ran his teams into the ground.

As the president and chief shareholder of Maple Leaf Gardens Limited, Ballard was worth over $100 million when he bought the Hamilton Tiger-Cats for $1.3 million in 1978. Ballard had made it no secret that the Toronto Argonauts were his first choice, but when he couldn't pry the team from John Bassett, he made a pitch for the Tiger-Cats instead. "I had nothing to do during the summer and wasn't prepared to sit around and watch the sky stay up."

Six years earlier, at the age of 69, Ballard had been found guilty of 47 counts of fraud and theft, that involved diverting $205,000 of funds from the Maple Leafs to support his lavish lifestyle. He served one year of a three-year sentence and came out of prison as cantankerous as ever.

When the local MP and cabinet minister, John Munro, opposed the sale of the team to Ballard, in part because of his less-than-stellar background, the response was typically insulting: "As far as Munro goes, he doesn't need to enter into anything I do. He's just a joke."

As a hated Hogtowner, Ballard was never accepted in Hamilton, even though he kept the team from folding by persevering through the lean years of the 1980s. During his 10 seasons as owner of the Ticats, average per game attendance dropped from 25,560 in 1978 to 14,756 in 1988. Ballard claimed he lost $20 million over those 10 years.

Despite losing more games than they won, Hamilton made the playoffs each year in the weaker Eastern Division and advanced to the Grey Cup for three straight seasons. In 1986, the Tiger-Cats upset the Edmonton Eskimos to win the Cup, the only championship that Ballard won in his years as an owner.

Al Bruno, the coach of the Ticats through most of those seasons, was a Ballard fan: "I loved the man. Ballard didn't stick his nose in like he did with his hockey team. If you did well, he rewarded you well. We won the Grey Cup in 1986. After that he gave me a three-year contract. He made us feel like we were somebody. They should have appreciated the man because he kept football going in Hamilton."

Throughout his ownership, Ballard fought with the city of Hamilton, especially over the condition of Ivor Wynne Stadium, one of the oldest in the league. "It is the worst stadium in the league, so there should be the worst attendance," claimed Ballard at one point when he owed $300,000 in back rent. "You get your ass full of slivers every time you sit down."

As attendance dropped each year, Ballard ran the team on a tighter and tighter budget. Harry Lappman, the team's public relations man, was forced to use a windowless storage room beneath the stands as an office. For some wacky reason only known to Ballard, Lappman was also forbidden to enter the press box during games.

Ballard also agitated the CFL head office by criticizing the Canadian game. He lobbied for adopting American rules and changing the field dimensions to match those of the game down south: "If the Americans made such a success of it, why the hell should we play something different?"

In 1980, during Grey Cup week, Ballard let loose with another anti-Canadian tirade, even though his Tiger-Cats were about to take on Edmonton in the championship game. "I now know there's no difference between the East and the West because we all get our supply of good players from the U.S. In fact, as soon as we get that damn rule changed so we don't have to play Canadians, we will be a hell of a lot better off," railed the crusty owner. "We shouldn't be penalized having to play guys just because they are Canadians. People pay a lot of money to see these games, and they deserve to see the best."

In 1989, Ballard battled his son Bill over control of his sports empire—a court case that included allegations that Ballard's son had assaulted his common-law wife, Yolanda. The next year, at the age of 86, Ballard died of kidney failure.

A decade earlier, he had been asked how he wanted to be remembered. "I don't want anybody to remember me," he had said. "I just do it myself while I'm here and remember myself."

The Pez

When he became the team's owner in 1989, Murray "The Pez" Pezim brought a larger-than-life profile to the BC Lions. The 68-year-old stock promoter had won and lost several fortunes over his business career and took another big gamble when he bought a Lions team that no one else wanted.

"I'm a promoter, pure and simple," said Pezim when he took over the team. "I've gone broke many times just because I won't quit, but I don't mind a bit."

The Pez was on a winning streak when he obtained the Lions. He had become a multi-millionaire after being awarded a huge financial windfall in an Ontario court ruling that involved his gold-producing company, Corona Corporation. He was about to marry wife number four, a 27-year-old beauty named Tammy Patrick. The two had just moved into a $7-million Vancouver mansion. When BC Premier Bill Vander Zalm asked Pezim to save the franchise, it would be a major test of the promoter's golden touch. The organization was a mess—even though there had been a mid-season coaching change, the team had still lost 11 games and was about to miss the playoffs for the first time in five seasons, the fan base was quickly shrinking, and the club had big bills to pay.

The Lions had operated under community ownership since they came into the league in 1954, but they now had a debt load of about $9 million. Pezim bought the team for $1.7 million and established a $2 million line of credit with the CFL.

For a short time, the kookiness of the Pez was a welcome diversion at BC Place. From the owners box, he did his best to entertain the crowd, including stripping to his waist after the Lions scored, waving his shirt and throwing it into the crowd. In the off-season, he signed ex–New York Jets defensive end Mark Gastineau not only to suit up for the Leos, but also to become, under Pezim's guidance, the world heavyweight boxing champion.

At a memorable press conference, Gastineau and his girlfriend Brigitte Nielsen—who had been previously hooked up with Sylvester Stallone—informed the media that she was pregnant and that they both had tattoos on their bums, each with the other's name. Gastineau, Nielsen and Gastineau's father (a former pro boxer) were all named to the Lions' board of directors. Nielsen was put in charge of "women's operations."

Gastineau only suited up a short time in BC. He did block a field goal in his first game with the Leos, but only lasted three more contests before he was released because of injuries. Gastineau gained most of his notoriety in a Lions uniform when he was involved in a wild, helmet-swinging brawl. He did manage to win 15 of 17 boxing matches against a run of severely limited opponents, however.

A short time later, Pezim announced that ex-Lions quarterback Joe Kapp would run the team. Kapp had been a legend in Vancouver, the on-field leader who had brought BC their first Grey Cup in 1964. At the same time, Pezim also hired Larry Kuharich, an old school, tough-guy coach to take over on the field.

Two assistant coaches resigned early in Kuharich's stint as a field boss. After a 2–7–1 start, Kuharich himself was fired; Kapp was let go a short time later. Kapp had made a significant signing when he lured quarterback Doug Flutie away from the NFL. After taking a year to learn the nuances of the CFL game, Flutie led the Lions to an 11–7 record in 1991 and a playoff appearance. The team still lost $2.5 million.

In 1992, Flutie left BC to sign as a free agent with the Calgary Stampeders. Without their star quarterback, the Lions lost their first seven games of the new season. Pezim walked away, leaving the league to run the team for the remainder of the campaign.

"It's no fun at all," said the dejected promoter. "It was fun for a while, even when we were losing money. But now we're losing, and people are laughing at me. I don't like being laughed at."

The roller-coaster life of Pezim had spiralled to the bottom. When Pezim dumped the Lions, the stock market was in the sewer, the superintendent of brokers in the province was trying to shut him down, Tammy was long gone and the Gastineau-Nielsen romance (and Gastineau's boxing career) was over.

The Three Amigos

At the time it seemed like the perfect marriage. The Toronto Argonauts, the team playing in Canada's biggest market, needed a major boost. To the rescue came a trio of owners who promised to bring some razzle-dazzle to a losing franchise.

Bruce McNall ("the rich one"), an entrepreneur and promoter from Los Angeles who had brought Wayne Gretzky to Hollywood and made the Kings the hottest sports ticket in town, led the charge. McNall recruited his friend John Candy ("the funny one") to throw in $1 million (of the $5.5-million purchase price) to become a 20-percent owner of the team. The comedian was a transplanted Canadian with a deep love of the CFL. And finally, McNall also talked Gretzky ("the great one") into buying a piece of the Argos.

The Ontario native brought instant credibility to the ownership group.

At the introductory press conference in February 1991, McNall and company promised to turn around a mediocre football team that was languishing in the enormous SkyDome. McNall had turned around the LA Kings with the acquisition of Gretzky and was convinced a bold move or two would revive the ailing football franchise.

A few months later, Argo fever began when the new owners signed the biggest name in U.S. college football, Notre Dame's Raghib "Rocket" Ismail, to an $18-million contract. At the home opener, Candy recruited Dan Ackroyd and Jim Belushi (replacing deceased brother John) to perform in a special Return of the Blues Brothers concert at halftime. Hollywood stars Mariel Hemingway, Martin Short and Dave Thomas also showed up at the Dome. There were marching bands and lots of special effects, and a crowd of 41,000 came out to witness the excitement.

Candy became a tireless promoter of the team and the league. It wasn't unusual for the overweight entertainer to show up at radio stations in Edmonton, Regina and Winnipeg to bring some hype to upcoming games. "He was wildly creative, and for a while he seemed to be practically running the CFL," recalled Brian Cooper, the

Argos' chief operating officer at the time. "He would devote endless hours, attend almost every game, go to meetings of the board of governors. We'd go to Edmonton on a small private plane. He'd try to break the blackout rule, he'd do a media blitz like you would not believe, and he'd be with the players during meal breaks, offering encouragement."

Led by quarterback Matt Dunigan and the Rocket, Toronto became the most improved team in the league. The Argos easily won the Eastern final over Winnipeg to advance to the Grey Cup. On a snowy field, Toronto capped off the miracle season with a 36–21 win over the Calgary Stampeders.

It was dream come true for Candy. As a kid he had played football on his Toronto high-school team and watched the Argos at Exhibition Stadium. For the better part of a year, the comedian put his career on hold to cheer on his hometown football team. "Controlling him on the sidelines was probably the biggest problem we had," explained Mike McCarthy who was then the team's GM and vice-president of football operations. At one point Candy ran onto the field to help an injured Argos player to the sidelines. "The referee gave me a dirty look," recalled

McCarthy. "I hollered at him, 'What do you want me to do about it? It's John Candy!'"

But even during that stunning season, the Argos were losing money, big money—more than $3 million in 1991 alone. As the losses mounted, McNall began to pull back. Toronto started trading its star players to save money, and Ismail headed to the NFL after two seasons. The Argos even sold the rights to the 1993 Grey Cup to Calgary in return for cash.

McNall was desperately trying to keep the team afloat as creditors moved in. Gretzky wanted out. Three years after buying the team, McNall put the for-sale sign on the Argos. Labatt's/TSN bought the team, much to the dismay of Candy, who was trying to put together his own group to purchase the team. A few years later, it was revealed that McNall had defrauded a host of American banks of more than $200 million. The LA entrepreneur subsequently served a four-year sentence in a U.S. prison before being released in 2001.

A few weeks after the sale of the Argos was announced, Candy died of a massive heart attack while shooting a film in Mexico. He was only 43 years old. In 2007, the CFL recognized the contributions of both Candy and Gretzky to the league by adding their names to the Grey Cup as part owners of the championship Argos squad (only McNall's name had been etched on the Cup).

John Candy would have been honoured that his contribution to the Argos' success had been immortalized on the Grey Cup. Joe Flaherty, one of Candy's friends and former colleagues with the Second City TV comedy troupe, summed it up: "He's deserving of it, too. I really think he was instrumental in helping to keep the CFL going at the time. He got a lot of publicity for the team and for football."

After McNall was released from prison, the Hollywood community stepped in to help with his financial recovery. A company called Fine Arts Entertainment hired McNall to help cast talent, hire directors and arrange financing for new movies. In the 1980s, he produced two profitable films (*WarGames* and *The Fabulous Baker Boys*) and was still well connected in the industry. He finished serving his prison term still owing the U.S. government $5 million—almost a half of every paycheque he receives still goes to settle that debt. The money is used to provide financial restitution to the victims of his financial shenanigans.

Despite the time in prison and the millions of dollars he has had to pay to the government,

McNall seems unrepentant to the financial hardship he caused his former associates and employees. He claims his intentions were good right up to the end: "I always thought we could fix the problem."

Calgary's Mr. Flamboyant

During the early 1990s, Bruce McNall was not the only CFL owner making headlines by throwing a lot of money around. In 1992, Larry Ryckman, a stock promoter from Calgary, bought the money-losing Stampeders and promised to turn the franchise into a winner.

Ryckman's first big move was to lure quarterback Doug Flutie away from the BC Lions. The owner of the Ryckman Financial Corporation signed the CFL's best player to a contract for $1.1 million per year that included 10-percent ownership in the Stampeders. Over the next four years, Calgary was the league's best team, setting 27 CFL records. The Stampeders won the 1992 Grey Cup in Ryckman's first season as owner.

Ticket revenues soared with the Stampeders' success, but Ryckman was a free spender, paying his players above the CFL average, refurbishing McMahon Stadium with skyboxes and losing

$2.4 million in hosting the 1993 Grey Cup. He was a hometown hero who had saved the team from the brink of insolvency, and in the process, Ryckman became one of most influential executives in the CFL.

Much of the money Ryckman had pumped into the team was borrowed, and in 1996, the house of cards began to cave in. The Alberta Securities Commission ruled that Ryckman had illegally manipulated the stock prices of his company, Westgroup Corporations. He was fined $492,000, an amount later reduced to $250,000. Then a long list of creditors began lining up for their money.

Alberta Treasury Branches was owed $8.6 million, the provincial government another $3.5 million. Flutie claimed he was due $833,000 in unpaid salary. Throw in unpaid bills to the CFL, the CFL Players' Association, Revenue Canada and Phoenix Press, and Ryckman owed in excess of $12 million.

Bankruptcy proceedings decimated the Stampeders front office as 14 employees were axed. Season-ticket holders also lost the $750,000 they had paid out in advances for the 1996 season, money Ryckman said was used to cover Calgary's operating costs. Flutie's salary was shed when he signed a two-year deal with the Toronto Argonauts in 1997.

Through all the financial turmoil, Ryckman remained upbeat about his future. "I'm eating humble pie today, but I'll be back bigger and better than ever," he said. "I'm 36 years old, and I'm gonna go out and earn a lot of money again."

Calgary Sun sportswriter Eric Francis summed up the Ryckman legacy: "He saved football, but the bottom line is he stiffed a lot of people. Still, the Stampeders are now one of the cornerstones of the league all because of Larry Ryckman. It's very sad that may not be remembered."

The Crazy House of Feterik

In his three-and-a-half year reign as owner of the Calgary Stampeders, Michael Feterik left many lasting images for the team's fans to remember.

At first things went pretty well. Head Coach Wally Buono had handled the Stampeders as head coach and general manager for 13 seasons, making the playoffs in 12 of those years. Calgary had won the Grey Cup in 1992, 1998 and 2001. With Buono running the football side of things, Feterik got to hold the Grey Cup in his first six months as the Stamps owner after Calgary won the 2001 championship. Chaos, however, was looming even during Grey Cup week. Buono was in his option season, and the question hanging over the franchise was whether Buono would stay in Calgary or start looking elsewhere. A sense of disconnect within the team surfaced at one press conference. While Feterik was telling reporters that Buono was free to shop his services around the league, only a few feet away, the new chief operating officer, Fred Fateri, was informing other general managers to back off.

It was just the start of downhill journey for an organization that had been the league's steadiest franchise. One overriding question was, Why did a highly successful businessman from California who had made a fortune selling cardboard boxes want to take over a Canadian football team in the first place? The answer was simple: Buono had signed Feterik's son Kevin as a third-string quarterback.

Kevin Feterik had been a star at Brigham Young University. Buono had a knack for bringing along young quarterbacks and turning them into successful professional players. The youngster had been with the Stampeders for a couple of seasons, and his father felt he was ready for a bigger role on the team.

The writing was on the wall, so, when the BC Lions came courting in 2003, Buono knew it was time to leave Calgary. "Mike bought the club and wanted his own coach who'd do what he wanted to do," explained Buono, number two behind Don Matthews in all-time CFL coaching victories. "We were never going to be on the same page, and it was his team, his money."

With Buono gone, Fateri hired Jim Barker, the offensive coordinator from Montréal to run the team. It was the first in a chain of misadventures that resulted in three straight losing seasons. Kevin Feterik was named the team's number-two quarterback behind Marcus Crandell, a still-untried CFL commodity. The owner's son had the smarts for the position, but not the arm strength for the longer and wider CFL field. He was also on the slim side and was pounded on more than one occasion by opposing defenders. During one ill-advised start, television cameras caught Feterik's mother holding him on the sidelines after a defensive lineman had knocked him into la-la-land.

Barker was squeezed by management to continue giving the owner's son more playing time, while defending the results on the field. When asked how difficult it must be for the younger Feterik to succeed in such a pressure-packed situation, Barker replied: "Any Catholic kid who steps right in at Brigham Young University, when 65,000 fans want a Mormon in there, has been through this before."

Then there were the exploits of Fateri, Feterik's right-hand man. Fateri was a banker with no previous experience in football, and it showed. The Calgary press was given plenty of fodder by his antics: running down the sidelines in an Armani suit and Italian loafers, high-fiving players while reaming out the officials, boasting on a radio talk show that he could bench-press 300 pounds and challenging a local sports columnist to a boxing match. Fateri also liked to brag about how he had been expelled from five European boarding schools when he was a kid.

In 2003, Feterik announced that Mark McLouglin, the team's kicker, would become the new president of the Stampeders. The long-time place-kicker stayed on the job for all of 56 days before declaring that his work had been completed. "Part of my plan was to try and put this organization back on the right track," said McLoughlin who went back to field-goal kicking while still the team's president. "I just didn't know how long it was going to take to execute our plan," McLoughlin said. "We were able to do it in a couple of months."

No one was quite sure how things had changed during McLoughlin's brief tenure. Fateri had resigned as COO, but at least a dozen players were ready to leave the Stamps at the end of the 2003 season, discouraged with the constant meddling of ownership, especially at the quarterback position where Kevin Feterik had become the number-one guy.

In 2004, the Stamps finished at the bottom of the CFL with a 4–14 record. Matt Dunigan, a CFL legend at quarterback, had been lured from the broadcast booth to become both the GM and head coach, despite having no experience running a team or drawing up Xs and Os. Under Feterik, the club had fielded three head coaches, three general managers and three presidents and had posted a 15–39 record.

By 2004, the Feterik had finally had enough and asked CFL commissioner Tom Wright to help find a buyer for the club. A new ownership group stepped forward at the beginning of 2005. Feterik insisted he had enjoyed his time as the owner of football team. "It was fun. It's just 'this' about Kevin and 'that' about Kevin just beats you to death. You get disenchanted. But as time goes on, I don't hold any grudges," said Feterik. "I just tried to help out where I could. It just didn't work. Things went south and we moved on."

John Forzani, an offensive lineman with the Stamps in the 1970s was part of a 12-member group that paid a record $6.1 million dollars to take over control of the team. Forzani could not believe what had gone on in Calgary: "The field-goal kicker becomes the CEO? Please, this is elementary school. You don't do that. What do you think if you've laid $400 down for a season ticket? One of two thoughts hits your mind. One, it's such an easy job that just about anybody can do it. Or two, the guy pulling the trigger is absolutely out of his tree."

Despite all the turmoil through Feterik's time at the helm, he was on the field when Calgary won the Grey Cup: "I was officially the owner when we won," he said. "You can't take that away from me. I've got the ring."

Nelson Skalbania

At the peak of his success in the 1970s, Nelson Skalbania was flipping commercial real estate worth $500 million a year. He also owned, at various times, six professional sports franchises, including the Montréal Alouettes. Skalbania was most famous as the guy who signed Wayne Gretzky to his first professional contract in Indianapolis for the World Hockey Association, later trading him to the Peter Pocklington–owned Edmonton Oilers.

Skalbania was born in Saskatchewan but spent his teenage years in Vancouver. His family was so poor that Nelson had to skip school on the days his clothes were being washed because he had only one pair of pants. He persevered to get a civil engineering degree at the University of BC, but was drawn to the business world, especially real estate.

Over time, Skalbania became a master negotiator and the king of the flip. He was always playing on the edge, relying on the inflation of the 1970s to keep the value of his assets increasing, even though many of them had a negative cash flow. In *Maclean's* magazine, Peter C. Newman described Skalbania as having a sweet and appealing side: "The habitual gambler in him is hostage to another, more rational and charming self, a man of good humour and surprising compassion who regards business as a lark and the world as a giant windmill to tilt against."

Skalbania bought the Alouettes in 1981 and made an immediate splash in Montréal when he signed four NFL stars to contracts: quarterback Vince Ferragamo, a starting QB in Super Bowl XIV with the Los Angeles Rams in 1980 was paid

$300,000 a year, a huge amount for a CFL deal; receiver James Scott; kick returner Billy "White Shoes" Johnson; and running back David Overstreet. Ferragamo was a bust, returning to the NFL after just one season. The team finished with a laughable 3–13 record, but still qualified for the playoffs, where they lost 20–16 to Ottawa in the Eastern semifinal. Skalbania lost $2 million in his first season, and with his empire crumbling around him, the league stepped in to revoke his ownership. The Alouette franchise was laid to rest, and a new Montréal team, the Concordes, joined the CFL.

Montréal fan Andy Nulman captured the craziness of the 1981 season by providing the lyrics to a country-flavoured song:

Vince "the prince" Ferragamo
had all the hero assets,
good looks and endless charms.
Too bad most of his passes
met opposition arms.
You'd figure these new players
would make Als-watching fun.
The only thing that thrilled us so
was the bang of the game-end gun.
Jim Eddy then replaced him,
promised changes at all cost,
The only real change in the next game was

the score by which they lost.
The fans they started faithful.
They roared like grizzly bears.
Before long they were showing up
disguised as empty chairs.

Earl Lunsford, the general manager in Winnipeg, said Skalbania was "the worst thing that ever happened to Canadian football." The Alouettes owner countered, "What did I do, rob someone? Murder this man? Did I hit anybody? Am I the villain for going broke writing cheques to keep football in Montréal? Why is everybody giving me hell for blowing my brains out?"

By the end of 1982, Skalbania's lifestyle and loose business ethics caught up with him. In a well-chronicled public episode, he apologized to his estranged wife Eleni in front of 400 guests at a party, by declaring, "I'll be the most honest, loving, considerate husband possible. I just have to get rid of all the shackles that are draped over my skinny shoulders."

His plea worked, and the couple later reconciled, even though later that same evening he announced he was $39 million in debt. Instead of declaring bankruptcy, however, his creditors let him work out his debts. Bankers actually lent him more money to carry out a number of crazy ventures including setting up a pirate radio station off the English coast, purchasing a moth-balled cruise ship, a Beatles museum, a resort called Club West that marketed horses instead of beaches and an Australian aerospace firm that launched satellites.

By 1996, there were 61 civil suits piled up against him, and he was charged with fraud, theft and forgery. He briefly owned the BC Lions the same year, but with his financial health failing, he was forced to hand over control of the club to a receiver after only six months.

In 1997, the BC Supreme Court sentenced him to one year in jail for stealing $100,000 from a prospective real-estate partner. Instead of depositing the money in a trust account, Skalbania had used the funds to pay off a $50,000 debt to another financier and for payments to his daughter and to a brokerage firm.

The bearded sports magnate avoided jail time when a number of prominent friends intervened by providing character references and by testifying on his behalf. The court instead sentenced him to a year on parole wearing an electronic ankle bracelet that allowed corrections officials to monitor his every move.

After his parole was completed, Skalbania went back to work, though with a much lower profile. He continues to work behind the scenes to finance real estate projects, including an $800 million ski and golf resort between Vancouver and Whistler, and is involved in a New Mexico company researching ways to desalinate sea water using solar energy.

The Gliebermans

It's not very often in the annals of sports history that owners are so incompetent that they utterly destroy two professional sports franchises playing the same sport in the same city in the same league.

Flashback to the late 1980s. After three decades of stable management and competitive teams, the Ottawa Rough Riders were a struggling franchise. CHUM Radio owner Allan Waters had lost $13 million in the nine years he had owned the Rough Riders, and he ended up unloading the team to a group of local businessmen for one dollar when he couldn't find another buyer. The new operation was severely undercapitalized, and the team lost another $2.5 million in two seasons.

In 1991, the six remaining directors of the team resigned and left the franchise in the hands of the league. It cost the CFL another $3 million to keep operating the Rough Riders, but a few months later, the team was purchased by Detroit real-estate developer Bernie Glieberman. His 23-year-old son Lonie was named club president. The Gliebermans were not obligated to pay any of the outstanding debt the team had accumulated.

At the time, it was hard to believe that the tumultuous ride the Ottawa fans had suffered for so many years could become an even wilder roller-coaster trip with a few tracks missing and brakes that didn't work. The Gliebermans were meddlers, not content to let their management, coaches and staff run the show.

General Manager Dan Rambo had been following a careful blueprint to bring the team back to respectability, but in 1992, the Gliebermans signed Dexter Manley, a former NFL all-pro defensive lineman. Manley had retired from football after the NFL suspended him for life when he broke the league's substance-abuse policy on four separate occasions. The move did not sit well with Ottawa fans, the media or Rider players.

Manley arrived in Ottawa out of shape and uninterested in playing. The locker room fell apart, and rifts developed among the players.

Lonie Glieberman was more interested in chasing cheerleaders and even managed to get into a downtown bar brawl.

At mid-season, the Gliebermans brought in J.I. Albrecht to act as a consultant for football operations, undermining Rambo's position even more. In late August, Albrecht convinced Bernie Glieberman to start Manley ahead of a veteran all-star player. Two assistant coaches resigned in protest. Following the season, head coach Rod Smeltzer was fired and the remaining coaching staff was let go.

Throughout the season, the Gliebermans had relentlessly nagged the city of Ottawa to renegotiate the terms of their rental deal to play in Frank Clair Stadium. When the city council wouldn't budge, Bernie Glieberman announced that he would be seeking to move the team to another city.

CFL commissioner Larry Smith replied that the 118-year-old franchise wouldn't be moving anywhere, but agreed to let Glieberman purchase a new team if he could find a buyer for the Rough Riders. When local businessman Bruce Firestone came to the rescue, the Gliebermans announced a new franchise in Shreveport, Louisiana.

Not surprisingly, Bernie and Lonie made several demands on Louisiana city and state governments. Shreveport's 40,000-seat Independence Stadium needed $8 million in renovations, and the state was to pay $2.5 million. The stadium lease with the city was for 10 years at a per-game cost of only $2500.

Shreveport welcomed the team, and the local newspaper claimed it as a "monumental moment in local sports history and in the community's history." Lonie Glieberman bragged that the Shreveport Pirates would be the first U.S. franchise to win a Grey Cup.

The Pirates lasted two seasons, winning only a handful of games before ever-shrinking crowds. The Gliebermans took another $3.5-million loss before the team folded. It seemed at last that the family had had enough of football.

Meanwhile in Ottawa, things only got worse. Firestone lost more money with the Rough Riders and wanted out. In 1995, a Chicago restaurant owner named Horn Chen took over the team. Chen only lasted a year. With only 3000 season-ticket holders left, he simply stopped funding the team. Once again the league took over, but after losing another $1.8 million running the Rough Riders while looking for new ownership, the league folded the 120-year-old sporting institution in 1996.

Professional football returned to Ottawa in 2002. The long decline of the Rough Riders had caused so much bitterness in the city that the new franchise was renamed the Renegades. But the name change did not bring the team any better luck, and for the next four seasons, the new team struggled on the field as much as the old one had, losing more than twice as many games as they won.

Attendance became an issue and, therefore, so did money. In 2005, Bernie Glieberman returned to the CFL, buying a majority ownership of the Renegades. As before, his son Lonie was named the team's president. The Gliebermans had spent their time out of football operating a ski resort in Michigan called Mount Bohemia. There, Lonie had tried out some creative marketing campaigns on the ski hills that he couldn't wait to bring back to Ottawa.

Lonie announced that the Renegades would run a new promotion called Mardi Gras Madness for home games throughout the season. Adapted from the Mardi Gras festival in New Orleans, women seated in the south-side upper deck only—traditionally the rowdiest part of Frank Clair Stadium—were encouraged to collect beads from men, which on Bourbon Street is achieved by flashing breasts. The woman with the most beads would be awarded $1000.

Belatedly realizing that there would be a number of children and their parents in the stands, the club revised its policy before the home opener in July to forbid nudity. Flashers were to be escorted from the premises. This happened on a regular basis during the first four home games. On one occasion, police and security people were pelted with hotdogs and beads as they escorted one young woman out of the park. Glieberman promised that anyone offended by the promotion would be allowed to exchange their seats for a different section in the stadium. About 100 people were relocated.

Ottawa city councillor Jan Harder led the charge against the dubious promotion. Surprisingly, she decided to take the low road in her criticism of Mardi Gras Madness by disparaging Lonie's physical stature and masculinity on a local radio station. She vowed to use whatever bureaucratic means possible to close down the party.

Glieberman stuck to his guns, however, insisting that the promotion was a fun and harmless way to spice up the atmosphere inside the stadium. Mardi Gras Madness, as well as the controversy, rolled on through the summer, with the police continuing to eject the more exhibitionistic competitors. Nevertheless, in late August, the Renegades announced that the promotion would end. City officials and the CFL head office had combined to wear Lonie down. The city had also threatened to crack down on tailgating, a tradition in which fans arrived at the stadium early to barbeque and drink in the parking lot—in violation of the city's liquor laws. Once Mardi Gras Madness ended, though, the tailgating resumed without interference.

Chapter Four

On the Sidelines

Legendary coach Bud Grant, who won four Grey Cups with the Winnipeg Blue Bombers and then headed south to lead the Minnesota Vikings to four berths in the Super Bowl, described the ingredients required to become a successful coach: " A good coach needs a patient wife, a loyal dog and a great quarterback—but not necessarily in that order."

The CFL proved to be a successful training ground for Grant, and even as an American, he understood the significance of the Grey Cup to Canadian culture: "It was an event that everyone went to or was interested in. John Diefenbaker said the Grey Cup was the greatest unifying force in Canada, bringing East and West together."

After he left to coach in the NFL, Grant still had strong memories of his many trips to the Grey Cup: "The Super Bowl was such a media event that it wasn't the fans or the celebration that bothered you, it was the crush of the media that wore you out. You can handle the enthusiasm of the fans, but the media crush was heavy and constant. The Grey Cup was more fun."

Like Grant, Marv Levy established his coaching pedigree in Canada before heading to the NFL and finding further success. In five seasons with Montréal, he compiled a 50–34–4 record, including two Grey Cup victories. Levy became a head coach in Buffalo, taking the Bills to four straight Super Bowl appearances. In all those visits, neither Grant nor Levy ever won a Super Bowl.

Four coaches—Lew Hayman, Frank Clair, Hugh Campbell and Don Matthews—are tied in all-time Grey Cup titles with five. Campbell was in charge of a dominant Eskimos team that won five straight Grey Cups between 1978 and 1982. No other team has won more than two consecutive championships since the Edmonton run. (In fact, only one team—the Toronto Argonauts in 1995 and 1996—has even won consecutive Grey Cups since then.) Campbell was only 36 years old when he took the job in 1977. His philosophy was simple: get the best players and let them make decisions on the field even if it results in the odd mistake.

There have been coaching and general manager standouts on every team. Ralph Sazio was a fixture in Hamilton, coaching the team to three Grey Cups. From 1968 to 1981, he moved from the sidelines to a desk job. As GM and then president, the team missed the playoffs only twice in 13 years.

Wally Buono has already been to the Grey Cup eight times as a coach and general manager, winning four titles—three in Calgary and one in BC. With a 227–112–3 coaching record, he is poised to overtake Don Matthews (231 victories) as the all-time CFL win leader.

The Water Boy

Bobby Ackles' story is a true rag-to-riches tale. In his memoir, *The Water Boy*, Ackles described his rise from poverty and neglect to become one of the most respected executives in all of professional football. He was born in Sarnia, Ontario, in 1938 and grew up in a nearby farming community called Locust Hill. His father earned money in construction, while his mother operated a truck stop, selling coffee and sandwiches from their house.

In the spring of 1952, Ackles' father took out an atlas and said it was time to pull up stakes. He had heard there was work in Vancouver, so, after selling most of their belongings, the family drove across country to the West Coast. They had a challenging start in their new province. At first, they couldn't find adequate housing and for two months had to camp out in Stanley Park, where the police would arrive every few weeks to move them on. The Ackles would then pack up, load up the car and find another spot to squat. The times were tough—Ackles' father struggled to find work, while his mother coped with three kids and another pregnancy. Finally Ackles' dad found a steady job, and they moved into a small house.

Despite the hardships, Bobby Ackles gained friends and acceptance by playing every sport he could fit into his schedule. There wasn't much family cohesion in the Ackles household, and sports provided the direction that Bobby needed to keep his life in order. Hockey and football were his two passions. To earn money, he scraped the ice at local rinks. In 1953, he read in a newspaper article that a new professional football team was starting in the city the following season. Ackles decided it would be great to be the water boy.

When the BC Cubs (the name was later changed to the Lions) held their first practice, Ackles walked up to the team's coach and general manager, Annis Stukus (nicknamed "the Loquacious Lithuanian") and asked if he could be the water boy. The CFL legend looked at the scrawny kid and said, "Come on. I'll put you to work."

It was the first day of a 40-year relationship that Ackles would have with the BC Lions, starting as the team's water boy and ending up as the organization's president and CEO. On that incredible journey, he served as the equipment manager, director of football development, assistant general manager and then general manager. He was part of three Grey Cup Championships along the way.

His first stint with the Lions lasted 34 years. But after winning the Grey Cup in 1985, Ackles, then general manager of the Lions, left BC—the result of an internal battle with the team's board of directors—and accepted a job offer from legendary Tex Schramm, the president and general manager of the Dallas Cowboys, to become vice-president of pro personnel. He helped put together a dynasty in Dallas; the Cowboys would win Super Bowls in 1993, 1994 and 1996. After shorter stints in the NFL with the Arizona

Cardinals, Philadelphia Eagles and Miami Dolphins and a brief stay in the XFL as general manager of the Las Vegas Outlaws, Ackles came back home to the BC Lions in 2002.

Ackles had a mess to clean up as the team's new president. When he left the Lions in 1986, the team had a solid season-ticket base of over 30,000 and regularly sold out the 56,000-seat BC Place Stadium. But poor ownership and management had left the Lions on the brink of bankruptcy until new owner David Braley had taken over the franchise in 1997. Still, despite winning a Grey Cup in 2000, the Lions were only averaging 18,000 fans a game.

Ackles went to work, luring Wally Buono from Calgary to become the team's new general manager and head coach. The team signed quarterback Dave Dickinson to lead the offence. Ackles reestablished the Lions' links to the community, and the team once again sponsored minor football in the city and took part in school programs. Players made appearances at community events throughout the year. Ackles also began forging ties with the business sector, securing the corporate support needed to make the team profitable.

Buono brought stability to the field and, led by Dickinson's savvy, the team became a league power. The team hosted three straight Western finals and won the 2006 Grey Cup. Fans began to come back to BC Place, and the season-ticket base edged up past 25,000. In his second stint with the Lions, Ackles began to receive the recognition he deserved as one of best executives in the history of the CFL. Tragically and unexpectedly, though, Ackles suffered a heart attack at the start of the 2008 season and passed away at the age of 69.

The Gender Bender: Jo-Anne Polak

When Jo-Anne Polak was named the general manager of the Ottawa Rough Riders in 1988, she became the first woman in CFL history to be appointed to an executive post. Little did she know that her three-year stint would become one long on-the-job-training session in crisis management.

The Riders, who were then owned by a 27-member community ownership group, had come off a dismal 2–16 campaign. In a surprise move, they named Steve Goldman and Polak as co-GMs. Goldman was assigned responsibility for the football operations, Polak the marketing of the team. The 29-year-old had a public relations and accounting background, but no experience in football.

Hard times had fallen on a once successful franchise. Home attendance had dropped to an average of 20,406, and the club was being run on a shoestring budget. Polak also had to withstand the sexist comments from her own football club executives and had difficulty gaining acceptance from her CFL colleagues.

Her appointment generated tons of publicity throughout the league, and she had to suffer the consequences of being in the public eye. After her first season, Polak disclosed that she had had four serious death threats over the course of the year.

"I've had my [telephone] number changed twice, and I get a lot of really obscene letters," said the rookie GM. "I've had people throw eggs and sandwiches and things like that at me. You spend a lot of time in cruddy bars doing a quarterback club [a team promotional event], where they all have tattoos and everybody wants to goose you or something."

The creepier part was dealing with infatuated admirers. "I live in a rural area, and I had a guy come out to the house, banging on the door and wanting to come in and have a Miller Lite beer," she said. "He had a scrapbook on me and knew everything about my parents. He had been to every single event I'd been to, taking pictures. It was weird. The police had to come and take him away."

Polak went to work in the 1989 season, putting together several successful promotional events that helped bring attendance up to 23,479. Behind the scenes, she was also trying to manage the backroom squabbling between members of the ownership group, while asking for financial help from local governments to keep the team afloat. Polak also built trust from the players by regularly updating the team captains on the Riders' financial situation.

The young general manager gained 30 pounds and suffered through countless sleepless nights trying to keep the team from folding. "You don't know what it was like to have $175,000 in the bank at 3:00 PM and then nothing by 9:00 PM," remembered Polak. "I'd constantly worry that if I screwed up, if I made the wrong decision, then I wasn't the only one who was going to suffer. I was going to drag down 75 families with me."

During the middle of the 1991 season, the Rough Riders' board of directors resigned en masse. The day after the board quit, the team's payroll was due, but a wire deposit was late, and

Polak didn't have enough money in the bank to cover it. Polak needed time to track down the money. In desperation, she called the coaching staff, who were still with the players, and told them to stall.

The coaches came through, breaking down more film as the players grumbled about the inexplicably long post-game meeting (the team had played Calgary the day before). By the time the tired Riders left Lansdowne Park, the money was in their accounts.

The CFL had to take over the club's operation, hoping to find a buyer before the team bled too much money from a league that was cash-poor. Polak was told she would be running both the football operation and the business side and that she would have to survive on a bare-bones budget. Her first decision was to fire Goldman (the team had lost four straight games to open the season).

"When I fired Goldman, people were saying, 'Who is she to do it? Who is she to decide?' Well, I'll tell you, a lot of this isn't as difficult as you might think. People would be surprised about how much I've learned about football."

Ottawa staggered through the season. The Riders players never complained about their situation, even though they suffered through winter conditions without capes and parkas to keep them dry. Polak finally went to the league and pleaded for $3500 to buy some capes to keep the players from freezing on the sidelines. The CFL commissioner, Donald Crump, finally agreed, but the team was not allowed to embroider the players' names on the back of the capes, just in case the Riders folded.

Late in the season, the league found new ownership, when Bernie and Lonie Glieberman from Detroit took over the franchise. The Gliebermans asked Polak to stay as the general manager, but, on the verge of burnout, she declined the offer.

The team only had an 18–36 record during her tenure, but Polak was proud of what she had accomplished in keeping the team alive: "All along, I honestly thought that I'd never be in a position to resign from this job. I always thought I'd leave because the team folded."

Polak had a half-dozen job offers waiting after she quit the Riders and decided to become a morning-show host with a local country-music radio station.

The Don

The most successful coach in CFL history is a complicated fellow. Don Matthews is certainly not an average senior citizen. He drives hot cars and dates women less than half his age. He's been the featured performer in a hip-hop video and tells off-colour jokes that make even football players blush.

"He'll never act his age," said Doug Peterson, a retired lineman who played under Matthews from 1999 to 2001. "The older he gets, the younger he gets. He'll always be a 17- or 18-year-old cocky kid."

Over the last three decades, Matthews has had 231 regular-season victories, tops on the all-time list. He has coached for 31 years in the CFL—21 as a head coach. In 18 of those seasons, his teams made the playoffs. He has won five Grey Cups as the head guy, five more as an assistant in Edmonton.

Football has been Don Matthews' life. He has moved around the CFL—six different teams, including three stints with Toronto and two turns with Edmonton. A hired gun, armed with ego and ambition, he has also been married and divorced four times along the way. "The same reasons I've been a successful coach have cost me in my personal life," admitted Matthews back in 1996, as he was preparing for yet another Grey Cup game. "Other people have been able to juggle it better. I immerse myself in the game, but I don't even know if I have a choice. It's who I am."

The Don, as he's been called for several years, has had furious encounters with the media—he won't tolerate what he thinks is a dumb question from a reporter. As a result of his adversarial exchanges with the media, TSN has refused to interview him on the sidelines during games. (In any case, the quality of his answers had declined into near grunts.) In rebuttal, he created a list of the top-10 clichés used by football coaches and vowed he would never use them.

Despite his adversarial relationship with the media, he has, at times, exploited the press to promote his concerns. In 2003, he turned the Grey Cup coaches' press conference into a sermon on treating coaches fairly. He was furious with the plight of former Toronto head coach Gary Etcheverry, who was fired with time remaining on his contract but was not paid because the team went into receivership. At the press conference, Matthews challenged the CFL to clean up its act. "After the league took over that franchise without a phone call, a letter or any communication, his salary was stopped," said the then Alouettes head coach. "And I'm not sure if that's a correct way to treat people in our positions of trying to better the league. We as head coaches have unified to the point of wanting to make it a public issue, a moral issue, not a legal issue."

Edmonton head coach Tom Higgins appeared uncomfortable sitting next to Matthews as he dominated the proceedings for 20 minutes and said later, "We all support what he was saying but it sure deadened the audience. It took us a while to get talking about the most important thing, which is the game."

CFL Commissioner Tom Wright was more biting in his comments about Matthews' stunt: "It is my hope we can now return our attention to football and the 91st Grey Cup."

The Don also exhibited his talent for flippancy during the 2004 "Spygate" controversy when he coached Montréal. Twice during the regular season, an Alouettes equipment volunteer, disguised as an Ottawa Renegades staff member, was found videotaping opposing coaches as they signalled players on the field during Renegades games at Frank Clair Stadium in Ottawa.

The Renegades and Blue Bombers protested after the first incident and, when Commissioner

Wright asked that the practice be discontinued, Matthews and the Alouettes replied that they would keep doing it until the league instituted a rule to stop it. Wright said the practice was "highly inappropriate" and warned Montréal to stop signal stealing.

Matthews said that the people who made this a serious situation were naive or not very knowledgeable about what goes on the pro sports world. "People in suits are way above me. I don't know half their names. They'll make 'suit decisions,'" he said in a shot at the league and the two protesting teams. "The preparation of my football team is consistent and thorough. It will continue."

The Alouettes organization was embarrassed by the scandal, but Matthews continued to supply tongue-in-cheek answers when the topic was raised during press conferences. When asked if he had employed signal stealing since his debut as a head coach in 1983, the Don replied, "Yes. And I've gotten better since then."

"It's the only reason we've ever won a game," he deadpanned. "Without stealing signals, Doug Flutie [his former QB in Toronto] would've been a bunch of crap."

And then there was Matthews' battle with his team's mascot in 2003. During a game between the Alouettes and Ottawa, "Blitz the Bird" drew a penalty for making contact with a referee on the sidelines. The Als were assessed a 10-yard penalty because of the actions of the gyrating fowl. Fortunately, the incident did not affect the outcome, as the Alouettes easily won 30–10.

Matthews wanted the bird to lose his job, but intervention by Als vice-president Mark Weightman saved the feathered mascot from the chopping block. "Blitz felt horrible afterwards," Weightman said. "He was simply trying to join in the end zone celebration after a touchdown and accidentally got too close to the ref. He sort of tried to smooth things over, but the ref probably saw this nine-foot-tall bird mocking him and threw the flag. Ironically, the person inside the suit is only five-foot-six."

"What Don does better than anyone else in CFL history is to win football games. He does that by controlling what happens on the field, which are the players. If something happens outside the realm of the team, well, I'd be pretty steamed, too."

After Matthews had cooled down the next day, he sent out a press release, advising the media that Blitz would be asked to a meeting with the head coach. The feathery mascot was told to bring along his playbook and reporters were invited to watch Matthews "tear a chicken strip off the whirly bird."

"Blitz and I have issues," said Matthews in the release. "The mascot will have to face his responsibilities."

In 2001, the demands of coaching took a physical toll on Matthews. In his third season with Edmonton, the then 62-year-old was forced to leave the team because of constant fatigue. His sudden departure was a shock to the franchise.

A year later, he was back in the league, this time with the Montréal Alouettes. He took a team that had a 9–9 record the previous year to 13–5 and a Grey Cup victory. Matthews has always loved the challenge of turning teams around in a short period. His greatest season as coach was in 1996 when he took Toronto from a 4–14 team to 15–3 and won the championship.

In 2006, Matthews walked away from the game again. Fourteen games into the season, he stepped down as the Als' coach because of anxiety. He retired to his home in Oregon to recover, and most CFL observers believed his coaching days were over.

Surprisingly, just over halfway into the 2008 campaign, the Don made another comeback. The Argos were struggling with a 4–6 record when Toronto general manager Adam Rita made a phone call to lure the 69-year-old north of the border once again. The move didn't work out as everyone hoped. The Argos lost eight straight games under Matthews' watch to miss the play-offs for the first time since 2001. Through the team's struggles, the head coach was upbeat, looked healthier than he had for years and claimed to be having fun.

Rita was hoping he could entice Matthews to return to Toronto in 2009, but after the season ended, the Don announced he was returning to his home in Oregon for good. In a 2006 interview, he said one of his goals in life was not to grow up or grow old. Matthews has admitted that the physical part is starting to catch up him, but that the fire still burns within: "I'm like an old man when I get into a boat, but my brain's not old. I don't consider myself old, and I don't want to act old. Away from football I'm more of a character than you'd imagine."

Chapter Five

The Players

For the most part, professional football players in Canada don't make much money. Until the 1980s, coaches scheduled practices late in the afternoon so their players could finish work at their day jobs before playing football.

Even these days, the average CFL player's salary is under $100,000. Only the league's top stars, mostly quarterbacks, earn over $150,000 per year. But the fans in the CFL tend to identify with the players who are making working-class salaries. They are accessible athletes, more approachable than professional players in other leagues.

In the past, CFL players tended to play in one city for their entire careers. They became part of the community. As in all pro sports, this happens less now, but the CFL still has an enviable list of sports icons who are identified with the cities they played in: Lui Passaglia, Tom Wilkinson, Normi Kwong, George Reed, Milt Stegall, Russ Jackson, Angelo Mosca, Pinball Clemens and Anthony Calvillo, to name a few.

And we all know that football players are tough. Edmonton centre Eagle Keys played most of the 1954 Grey Cup game with a broken leg. After being carried off the field in the first quarter in extreme pain, Keys inserted himself back in the lineup and continued to play until the discomfort grew so much that tears welled in his eyes.

In the 1989 Grey Cup, Hamilton receiver Tony Champion played most of the game with broken ribs but still caught eight passes for 106 yards. Late in the fourth quarter, he stretched out to make an acrobatic catch for a touchdown to tie the game at 40–40. The Roughriders eventually won 43–40 in one of the best Grey Cups of all time.

This chapter only partially lists some of the league's best performers, its most courageous athletes and some of its of craziest entertainers.

Dirty 30: Jim Young

Jim Young was called the dirtiest player in Canadian football. He acquired the nickname in 1967, his first season with the BC Lions, when he caught 46 catches for almost 1000 yards. He never objected to the moniker, declaring instead that, in football, dirty is a frame of mind.

In his 1974 book, *Dirty 30*, Young wrote that there are certain rules to playing the game on the edge, based on sanity and a desire to keep his body in one piece.

Rule 1: Never, ever hit anybody with a clenched fist. There are too many helmets and faceguards and shoulder pads to break your knuckles. The open-handed slap is just as effective and, with a good clothesline, you don't have to use your hand at all.

Rule 2: Never hit a defensive lineman unless you can hide behind your offensive linemen faster than he can get to you.

Rule 3: Hitting when they're not looking is much easier than hitting when they are. It's not cowardice; it's a fact of life. Besides, eventually they all get you back.

For his entire 13-year career, Young was a marked man and not just because he lived up to his nickname. He was also the best offensive player on some very bad Lions teams. Against Regina, one Roughriders coach would line up the middle linebacker opposite Young. He had one job: to follow the Lions' receiver around and beat the crap out of him.

Jim Young grew up in Hamilton, Ontario, a steel town with a reputation for producing tough football players. At that point, Young was an all-around athlete and an excellent student. His parents were members of the Brethren Church, a Quaker-like denomination with pacifist beliefs. His mother was appalled when her son chose football, while his father became a big fan.

When Young left home to attend Queen's University, he never returned to the church where he was raised. Because of that, his mother told him he was a Jonah and that his teams would never win. It ended up being a curse that held true—right up to his retirement in 1979, Young never played in a Grey Cup game.

After becoming the best college player in Canada, Young was drafted by Toronto, but was only offered serious money to play football with the Minnesota Vikings. After two seasons with the Vikings, the Lions traded two players, including all-Canadian defensive end Dick Fouts, to Toronto to get Young's rights. Then they traded

Joe Kapp to Minnesota for Young. It was a high cost to pay for a then unproven player, but Young ended up being a great investment, retiring as the Lions' all-time leading receiver.

"It isn't so much that he had great natural ability," summed up Eagle Keys, one of Young's head coaches with the Lions. "He's just always ready with what he has."

Challenging Pain: Matt Dunigan

How tough are football players? Matt Dunigan played for six CFL teams in his 14-year career, and for much of that time he played hurt—not just minor pulls and strains, but broken bones, swollen joints and concussions.

As a starter with the Edmonton Eskimos, he battled through a sprained left knee, scratched corneas in both eyes and a rolled ankle. The worst injury came when the bursa sac—a fluid-filled sac that lubricates joints—on his throwing arm was so swollen from his elbow repeatedly slamming into the turf that it looked like two eggs under his skin. In a game at BC Place, the elbow slammed into the artificial grass, bursting the skin on the elbow and leaving the bursa sac protruding a couple of centimetres through the hole. Dunigan went to the sidelines, where the doctor snipped off what was sticking out and sutured the skin back together, and the quarterback finished the game.

Even in the off-season, Dunigan had to battle pain. In December 1985, he had emergency surgery to remove his appendix. He was rushed through the anaesthetic procedure too quickly. On the operating table, he was paralyzed, but had complete awareness of his surroundings; he could feel the doctor cut him open and reach in with his index finger to take out the appendix. A week later, Young had to go back to the hospital when an infection set in; his stomach had a grapefruit-sized protrusion. It took him three-and-half months to recover, and he lost 26 pounds.

After two seasons in BC, Dunigan was traded to Toronto. He missed 10 of 18 games in an Argos uniform because of more injuries: a pulled groin, a pulled hamstring, a pulled calf muscle and a broken collarbone. After finally recovering late in the 1991 season, he took a hit that broke his collarbone in two places just before halftime in the Eastern final, which Toronto easily won 42–3 over Winnipeg.

Fast forward to Grey Cup week. Dunigan's throwing arm is in a sling, and there is much media speculation that he wouldn't play. The night before the 1991 Grey Cup, Dunigan, his father, Argos general manager Mike McCarthy and head coach Adam Rita, as well as the team doctors and trainers, huddle in a secret meeting in the ballroom of the Sheraton Hotel in Winnipeg. The team doctor has injected two pain blockers into Dunigan's shoulder, and now Dunigan has to convince everyone he will be ready to perform in about 18 hours. He tries throwing the ball. His first toss is to McCarthy, who is standing about 15 feet away. The throw lands five feet short. Then, as the painkiller releases into his shoulder, the Argos' quarterback is able to get more zip on the ball. Within minutes, he is able to throw the pigskin across the room without any discomfort. The decision is made that Dunigan will start the game.

"I talked to his parents. I talked to Matt. He talked to his wife," recalled Rita. "I talked to his doctor, who said there was no further damage that could be done. Basically, it was a decision made the night before the game. I had been told all week he wasn't going to play, so we had prepared Rickie Foggie."

The next morning, Dunigan was injected with two more shots of painkillers and a shot of adrenalin to get his muscles moving. It was a bitterly

cold Grey Cup in Winnipeg with the temperature at kickoff about −30° C with the wind chill
factored in. Between the medication and the
frigid conditions, Dunigan could barely feel his
limbs.

Toronto relied on their defence and special-
team play as the Argos' quarterback struggled
through the first three quarters. In the final
15 minutes, Dunigan threw two touchdown
passes to ice a 36–21 victory over Calgary. Toronto
team co-owner Wayne Gretzky called it one of
the gutsiest performances he had ever seen.

"He certainly sucked it up. He was tough, very
focused, a winner," echoed his Argo teammate
Dan Ferrone. "He brought a lot of qualities, definitely leadership skills. When he left after the
1991 season we missed him."

In 1993, Dunigan returned to the Grey Cup,
this time as a member of the Winnipeg Blue
Bombers. Unfortunately, a torn Achilles tendon
late in the regular season put him on the sidelines through the playoffs. The next season, he
suffered from plantar fasciitis in his heel. The
ligaments that stretched between the heel and
toes were ripping away from the bottom of his
heel. For the next 14 straight weeks, he had to
have a two-inch needle full of pain-killing

medication rammed into his heel to allow him to practice and play.

The most serious challenge Dunigan would face came in 1996 as a member of the Hamilton Tiger-Cats. After winning four of their first five games, the Ticats were facing the BC Lions at Ivor Wynn Stadium. In the first quarter, Reggie Carthon, a BC defender, blitzed from his left halfback position.

Dunigan never saw him coming. Carthon stuck his right shoulder into Dunigan's chest and ran right over the Ticat quarterback. The ball came loose on the play, and Dunigan's head snapped back into the turf. In a daze, he ran after the ball and jumped onto a pile of players. In the ensuing melee, Dunigan was peeled off the pile and thrown onto the turf again, hitting his head on the unforgiving artificial surface.

On the next Hamilton possession, Dunigan, still in a fog, insisted on going in again. On the second play, BC linebacker Sheldon Quarles applied a helmet-to-helmet hit that ended up being the final knockout blow to the quarterback's playing career.

Over his football career, Dunigan was diagnosed with concussions on 12 occasions, but he estimates there were probably double or triple that many. The gutsy quarterback still suffers from some of the symptoms of post-concussion syndrome—to this day, memories of past events pop out of what has become a sometimes foggy personal history.

The Stuke

One of the most colourful characters in CFL history, Annis "the Stuke" Stukus, broke into the CFL with Toronto in the mid-1930s. The story goes that the young Lithuanian played three years with the Argos before he knew that his teammates were getting paid, and it wasn't until 1938 that he nervously approached Toronto's management for $500 to suit up the next season: "I would have asked for dough before that, but I was afraid that they wouldn't let me play football. What would I have done if they wouldn't let me play?"

The 1938 Argos had won the Grey Cup before a then-record crowd of 18,778 at Varsity Stadium in Toronto. Red Storey had been the hero in the 30–7 romp over Winnipeg, scoring three touchdowns. Among the more famous members of the team, however, were the Stukus brothers— Annis, Frank and Bill. Earlier in the season all three had scored touchdowns in the same game: Bill passed to Annis for one; Annis passed to Frank for six more points; and Bill scored a pair of touchdowns on his own.

In 1949, Stukus was hired to run the new Edmonton franchise. At the time, he was one of the few Canadian head coaches in the league. With a budget of $45,000, Stukus began putting a club together, winning four games and finishing third. Known as the "Loquacious Lithuanian," Stukus was a born marketer, with a knack for staging promotions that brought in much-needed revenue. With the extra money, Stukus went east and brought back five Toronto players to bolster his team.

Head coach Stukus was also the Eskimos' place-kicker. He was so sure that he wouldn't get hit that he never bothered to wear pads or a helmet. He didn't even take off his gold wristwatch.

Early in the first season, Stukus trotted into the huddle before attempting a game-winning field goal and spoke to his teammates. "I said to the guys in the huddle, 'Fellas, you know I don't believe in fines for mistakes. But this wristwatch is worth 85 bucks, and if anything happens to it while I'm out here, each one of you will buy me a new one.' I kicked that field goal and won the game, which really helped us with season-ticket sales. That watch went through 39 football games without a scratch."

Stukus successfully put the Edmonton franchise on the map, compiling a record of 19 wins and 23 losses, as well as securing two playoff berths in 1950 and 1951. The next season, he returned to his sportswriting job at the *Toronto Star*.

In 1954, a group of Vancouver businessmen approached Stukus about starting a new team in British Columbia. After much persuasion, he was offered a three-year contract and 25 percent of any profits to run the show. Stukus earned every dollar as a one-man operation—general manager, coach, publicist and ticket salesman. In their inaugural season, the Lions were terrible, winning only one game, but they led the league in attendance in the newly completed Empire Stadium.

It rained so much that first season that the players were afraid of getting lockjaw in what turned out to be a swampy field in the new stadium. "Our gang took tetanus shots," recalled Stukus. "They put the wrong kind of grass in there, plus we had eight home games, and it rained—and I'm talking about rain—for six of them. The field was quagmire."

With a questionable on-field product, Stukus spent an unheard-of $5000 per home game on halftime entertainment in an attempt to bring women to the stadium. "I would say that when we were breaking attendance records, we had the highest concentration of women at a sports event anywhere in the world except for maybe Wimbledon tennis. We sold the game to the gals."

The strategy worked as the team tucked away over $200,000 in the bank. However, the fatigue of dealing with a meddlesome board of directors took its toll, and Stukus left the team to become the football editor for the *Vancouver Sun* newspaper.

The Earthquake

They called him the Earthquake for a reason. For six seasons, Calgary Stampeders fullback Earl Lunsford hammered into opposing defences.

"He didn't have great speed, but he had great balance," explained former Stamps general manager Rogers Lehew. "He ran low and he ran hard. He was a wrestler in college and that gives you great balance and body control."

The former Oklahoma State Cowboy joined the Stampeders in 1956, before spending two years in the U.S. military. He returned to Calgary in 1959, where he hit his stride as one of most dominant running backs in the CFL. In 1961, he became the first professional running back in any league to crack the mythical mile in rushing—1760 yards—when he bullied his way to 1794, a mark that stood until Willie Burden ran for 1896 yards in 1975.

In the 1960 Labour Day Classic against the Edmonton Eskimos, Lunsford displayed his power running in an 85-yard run that wore down an entire defence. "He broke that run into about a 25- or 35-mile-per-hour wind, and it was the slowest damn run I've ever seen in my life," remembered Lehew. "Two Edmonton players overran him and then came back and missed him head on."

We ran it back the next day in the film room," added George Hansen, one of Calgary's offensive linemen at the time. "We thought they had it on slow motion."

Lunsford retired after the 1963 season as the Stamps' all-time rusher with 6994 yards. He still holds the Calgary career touchdown record with 55. In 1962, he scored five touchdowns in a single game, a team record that still stands.

In 1968, Lunsford took over as the Winnipeg Blue Bombers' general manager. He ran the team for 15 years and oversaw their stadium's expansion from 22,000 to 32,000 seats.

"Earl was here when I first arrived in Winnipeg, and he made a big impact on this city and football club," said Bombers president Lyle Bauer. "He made a contribution as both a player and a general manager."

Lunsford was elected to the CFL Hall of Fame in 1983. He died in his home in Fort Worth, Texas, in 2008 at the age of 74.

The Other Rocket

In the early 1990s, the American press called Raghib "Rocket" Ismail the most famous draft dodger in Canada. Bruce McNall was the reason. After Ismail's wildly successful college football career at Notre Dame, Toronto Argonauts owner McNall lured Ismail north of the 49th parallel before the NFL draft with a three-year contract for $18-million that included $4 million up front. In signing Ismail to a deal that was astronomically out of proportion with the rest of the CFL salary structure, McNall was following a formula that had worked a few years earlier when he had made a blockbuster trade to bring Wayne Gretzky to the Los Angeles Kings. McNall was gambling that the young receiver could rescue the Toronto franchise in much the same manner that Gretzky had revitalized hockey in California.

But while Gretzky had already established himself as the best hockey player of all time and was a sports icon across North America before the trade, Ismail was just another unproven collegiate talent. During his first season in the CFL, the Rocket put together some impressive rookie numbers, though, catching 64 passes for 1300 yards while scoring nine touchdowns. The Argos advanced to the Grey Cup, where Ismail helped Toronto clinch the championship with an 87-yard kickoff return for a touchdown.

The young receiver also helped the Argos at the gate, as their attendance jumped from 30,500 to 37,120 a game. The $4.5-million paycheque Ismail was making didn't seem so out of line. "In the beginning," said Edmonton Eskimos GM Hugh Campbell, "he was an excellent signing. He got the attention Toronto needed. I'm not sure he returned the investment dollar for dollar that first year, but nobody in the league was laughing at McNall."

The Argos owner was actually only paying Ismail $110,000 a season to play football. The rest of his contract with McNall was a personal-services deal to become an ambassador of the CFL—to be the Wayne Gretzky of Canadian football.

That's when things started to break down. "He may not have understood his function," said McNall about the Ismail gamble. "We really wanted him, for the bulk of the money, to promote the CFL in general and the Argos in particular. I still think he has charisma, and there's no doubt about his football abilities. But it's fair enough to say there have been disappointments off the field."

During Grey Cup week, Ismail embarrassed the team by not showing up at a "Meet the Players" breakfast. A week earlier, he had been a half-hour late for a team practice at the Sky-Dome, saying that he had gone instead to the Exhibition Grounds where the Argos normally practiced. Quarterback Rickie Foggie shrugged off the Rocket's tardiness: "He sleeps more than anyone I know. He also runs faster than anyone I know."

The 1992 season was a disaster for Toronto. When the Argos couldn't sign quarterback Matt Dunigan to a new contract, the team sputtered, falling from first to last in the four-team Eastern division. Without a quarterback to get him the ball, Ismail's production dropped to 36 catches for 651 yards.

Ismail's impact on the team had faded, and fans were wondering why he was the top-paid player in the CFL. In his role as spokesman for the league, the Rocket also had an off-season. He stood up some writers and TV reporters, and he became unreliable in his promotional duties. The media reported that Ismail had ducked out of a charity function, claiming to be sick, only to be spotted at a rock concert the same night. An in-depth interview on a national television network was cancelled when he didn't show up.

McNall and his staff approached the Rocket several times about his lack of commitment as a promoter of the game. "I may have been late for some of them," Ismail admitted, "but I think I attended them."

After the 1992 season, McNall was looking to bring the Argos operating expenses back in line with the other teams (Toronto had lost $3.5 million in 1992). An economic downturn in the United States had put pressure on McNall's other holdings, and there were rumours that the former Hollywood producer was in big financial trouble, with his creditors closing in. Combine this with McNall's disappointment in the

Rocket's performance off the field, and it seemed the 23-year-old star's time in Canada was about to come to a premature end.

The Los Angeles Raiders, gambling on Ismail's availability after his time with the Argos had ended, had drafted him in the fourth round of the 1991 draft, and they were ready to step in with a contract offer. Subsequently, Ismail had a short stint in the NFL, playing both as a kick returner and as a receiver.

Red Storey

Roy Alvin "Red" Storey is perhaps best remembered as an NHL referee who became more famous after his retirement with his natural gift for making people laugh. What many people don't recall is that Red Storey made a significant impact in the CFL, first as a player for seven seasons, and then as an official for 12 more years.

Storey burst onto the Canadian sports scene in 1938. The 6'3", 200-pound redhead made one of the most dramatic Grey Cup appearances in the classic's history. With the Toronto Argonauts trailing the Winnipeg Blue Bombers 7–6 in the third quarter, Storey was thrown into the game after starter Doug McPherson was injured.

The 20-year-old rookie scored on a 28-yard run that put the Argos ahead 11–7. A few minutes later, the youngster intercepted a pass and ran it back 40 yards for another Toronto touchdown. On the next series, Toronto teammate Bob Isbister picked off another Blue Bomber pass at the Argos' two-yard line. Isbister then lateralled to Storey, who ran the length of the field before being knocked out of bounds on the one-foot line. Toronto scored on the next play, when another Argos running back took it into the end zone.

"I should have scored that touchdown, too, but after my long run, they thought I was tired so they ran another play," remembered the tall redhead many years later.

Later in the quarter, Storey did add a third touchdown, this time on a 20-yard run, as Toronto clobbered Winnipeg 30–7. The second-stringer had scored three touchdowns in less than 12 minutes and also added a nonscoring 102-yard run. Newspapers at the time called it the "greatest one man show in Cup history." To add to the folklore of Storey's great individual performance was that, after being carried off the field on his teammates' shoulders, he still had to hitchhike to his home to Barrie, Ontario, later that afternoon.

Word of his exploits travelled south of the border, and Storey received tryout offers from the NFL's New York Giants and Chicago Bears. But Storey has having too much fun and making too much money as a semi-professional to turn pro in any one sport (he had kept his amateur status while playing in the CFL). Besides winning a second Grey Cup in football, he was also a star basketball player with championship teams in Barrie, Ontario. He also played baseball in senior men's leagues and was offered a contract by the American League's Philadelphia Athletics. As if that wasn't enough, he was also a star in senior lacrosse in the east's top leagues.

Storey's athletic career was cut short by two knee injuries and a surgery that went sour. By the age of 24, his playing days were over. After moving to Montréal, Storey began officiating lacrosse, junior- and high-school level football and school hockey games.

The young man had the good judgment and easygoing personality to be a top official and was soon working CFL games. The NHL came knocking, and in 1950, he started a nine-year run as a hockey referee that included officiating in seven straight Stanley Cup finals between 1952 and 1958.

In 1959, Storey was working the opening play-off series between the Montréal Canadians and the Chicago Black Hawks. Storey chose not to call penalties against two Montréal players at key points in the deciding game, and Montréal was able to capitalize on this and win the series. Chicago fans went wild and littered the ice with garbage. After the game, NHL president Clarence Campbell criticized both Storey's competence and integrity.

The redhead immediately quit as a referee and started a new career that eventually led to his becoming a celebrity across the country. He first worked in sales and public relations for Seagram, later becoming a radio and TV commentator and then a talk-show host. Storey became a sought-after public speaker at thousands of events and refereed more than 2500 Oldtimers and other charity hockey games. He raised over $25 million for various causes. At every appearance his hearty, booming laugh never failed to win over the people attending.

"I love to see people laugh," summed up Canada's most famous referee. "I figure if I can take a scowl off a lot of faces, I'm better than a lot of doctors."

At the age of 80, Storey finally had to hang up his skates and turn in his whistle for good. He passed away in a Montréal nursing home in 2006 at the age of 88.

The Little General

When Ron Lancaster passed away in September 2008, the CFL lost one of its most durable symbols of excellence and sportsmanship. For over four decades, Lancaster was the best at what he did—as player, coach and broadcaster.

He was the CFL's best quarterback for 19 seasons—the Little General of the Saskatchewan Roughriders for 16 years—and retired as the league's all-time leader in passing yards (50,535), touchdown passes (333), pass attempts (6223) and completions (3384). Lancaster still holds the CFL record for most completions, passing yards and touchdowns in the playoffs. He also led Saskatchewan to 50 fourth-quarter, come-from-behind victories. In Vancouver, Lancaster was known as the Heartbreak Kid for his merciless ability to defeat the Lions in games in which they appeared to have victory wrapped up.

Lancaster grew up in Clairton, Pennsylvania, and played his college ball at tiny Wittenberg University in Ohio. He was short (5'5") and kind of dumpy-looking, which led the NFL to ignore his fearlessness and knack for exposing the weaknesses in opposing defences. Instead, he came north, joining the Ottawa Rough Riders in 1960. He split the quarterbacking duties with Canadian legend Russ Jackson and won a Grey Cup as a rookie.

Just before the 1963 season was set to begin, Lancaster was dealt to Saskatchewan for $500, on condition he not be traded back to another Eastern Conference team. In partnership with running back George Reed and receiver Hugh Campbell, the Roughriders developed the league's most feared offence. Lancaster was named the CFL's outstanding player in 1970 and 1976. He led Saskatchewan to its first Grey Cup title in 1966 and to five Western Conference championships (1966, 1967, 1969, 1972 and 1976).

"He was the greatest I ever saw," said George Reed of his teammate. "Other guys might throw a tighter spiral or run a little faster, but no one in this league thought the game better. Ronnie's football mind is what set him apart."

After retiring from the gridiron in 1978, Lancaster coached in Saskatchewan for two seasons. It was a tough transition. Without their on-field leader, the Roughriders struggled, and Lancaster's coaching record was an awful 4–28. Subsequently, he became a colour commentator on

CFL telecasts for almost a decade, teaming with Don Wittman to become the best football broadcasting team in Canada.

In 1991, Lancaster was lured back to the coaching ranks with the Edmonton Eskimos, winning another Grey Cup as the head coach in 1993. Five years later, he left the Eskimos to take over in Hamilton. Lancaster turned around a 2–16 team in Hamilton, getting them to the Grey Cup in 1998 and winning it in 1999.

Lancaster, a two-time Coach of the Year, retired from the coaching ranks with 142 wins—number five all time.

"The combination of what he did as a broadcaster, as a player and as a coach and as an ambassador the last few years...it is really unmatched in the amount of fans he has personally reached," summed up Edmonton Eskimos legend Hugh Campbell of Lancaster's achievements.

Lancaster passed away after a short battle with cancer at the age of 69. Tributes poured in from across the country, remembering his excellence as a player and coach, his generosity with fans and the excitement he brought to the game. The Toronto *Globe and Mail* printed several reminiscences from readers across the country. Judy

Roberts of Toronto was among the many fans that felt a special connection with the quarterback during his playing days:

Although I never had the privilege to meet Ron in person, he was a vivid presence in my household as I grew up. My mother was a devoted fan, so we faithfully watched any of his Saskatchewan games that were broadcast on TV. What I remember most was our despair as the 'Riders got further and further behind as the game went on and then our elation as Ron "suddenly" seemed to focus and would effortlessly lead his team to victory in the fourth quarter.

We would end up exhausted by the end of the game, curse him for not putting us out of our misery earlier in the contest, vow that we were not going to subject ourselves to the same roller coaster ever again—but next game, there we were, glued to the TV and ready to sink or swim with Ron once again.

The Magic Flutie

In a 2006 poll conducted by the television network TSN, Doug Flutie was named the greatest player in CFL history by a panel of ex-players, coaches and executives. Once called "America's Midget" by Chicago Bears quarterback Jim McMahon, and admittedly undersized in a game of giants, this quarterback overcame the stereotypes associated with his small stature to become the "Magic Flutie" in his adopted homeland north of the 49th parallel.

His journey to professional football started at Boston College, the only NCAA team to offer him a scholarship (but only after two other quarterback candidates had turned them down). He became an American icon in 1984 with a last-play Hail Mary pass to defeat the reigning national champions University of Miami in a nationally televised game. The play guaranteed him the Heisman Trophy for that year, but because of his small stature, he was only drafted in the 11th round by the Los Angeles Rams in 1985.

As a result, Flutie was only too happy to bolt to the USFL's New Jersey Generals instead after Donald Trump offered him a six-year contract for an unheard-of $8.3 million. The league folded a year later, but Flutie was picked up by the Chicago Bears, who had traded with the Rams to get his rights, and made his NFL debut with them. Unfortunately, things didn't work in out in Chicago or in New England a year later, and Flutie was released in 1989.

On the brink of leaving football behind forever, the little quarterback was lured north to Canada when BC Lions owner Murray Pezim signed him to a two-year personal-services contract. It took him a year to adapt to the Canadian game, but in 1991, the genius of Flutie erupted when he threw for 6619 yards, the most productive season by a quarterback in professional football history, and a league record 466 completions.

"We developed an offence around what Doug did best," said Bob O'Billovich, the Lions' head coach when Flutie joined the team. "We didn't ask him to stay in the pocket. We moved the pocket and took advantage of his running ability. With his great peripheral vision, Doug was like a point guard leading a fast break in basketball. There has never been a quarterback in our league who could scramble as well when he got into trouble."

After two seasons in Vancouver, Flutie moved to Calgary, accepting a $1-million-a-year offer, plus a 10 percent ownership stake in the Stampeders. He then won his second outstanding-player award and guided Calgary to a Grey Cup. In 1994, he threw 48 touchdown passes—a CFL record that still stands.

In 1996, Flutie moved to Toronto and turned the Argonauts into instant champions, winning back-to-back Grey Cups while compiling a 34–6 regular-season record. Before leaving to finish his career in the NFL in 1998, Flutie had almost rewritten the CFL record book. In his eight seasons in Canada, he won six regular-season MVP awards and was MVP in three Grey Cups. He threw for 41,355 yards and 270 career touchdowns. In 2007, he was the first American-born athlete to gain admission into the Canadian Sports Hall of Fame. At a press conference prior to the induction ceremony, Flutie had this to say:

This place [Canada] has a very special place in my heart. People down south always ask me, "Would you have preferred to stay in the NFL all those years?" And I say I wouldn't have changed it for the world.

I really feel at home up here. I feel accepted. A lot of people in the States thought I was Canadian, the way I waved the flag for Canada. Part of that is that I really appreciated the support I got up here from the fans. I was never second-guessed up here. The height thing...whenever I was playing in the States I had a chip on my shoulder. But up here I just had fun. So

when I went back I was always supportive and
flattering in my reviews.

When Flutie announced his retirement from
the New England Patriots in 2006, he ended
a professional career that lasted 21 years—nine
more than McMahon, the man who had pegged
the CFL's best-ever quarterback as too small to
play the game.

Russ Jackson: Last of the Great Canadian Quarterbacks?

Who was the last great Canadian quarterback
and when did he retire? The first part of the
answer is Russ Jackson. The answer to the second part of the question is depressing because
Jackson retired from the CFL in 1969. Since his
departure from the league after 12 terrific years
with the Ottawa Rough Riders, not one other
Canadian-born QB has come close to performing
at his level.

Jackson won three Grey Cups in 1960, 1968
and 1969 and was named the league's outstanding player on three occasions. He was a CFL
all-star three times and an Eastern all-star six
times. In 1969, he retired at the top of his game,
winning the Grey Cup and the game's MVP

award. His performance in the final was all the more amazing in light of the fact that he had separated his shoulder in the first quarter. Before the game, threats had been made on his life, and security guards were stationed in and around the stadium. Those were the days when the FLQ (*le Front de Libération du Québec*) was carrying out acts of terrorism, and all threats were taken seriously.

Jackson left the game with a team record for total career passing yards (24,952) that still stands today. After hanging up his cleats, he went on to coach for the Toronto Argonauts for two years. In 1974, he was inducted into the Canadian Football Hall of Fame.

Russell Jackson came to the CFL out of Hamilton's McMaster University and won a spot on the Rough Riders roster as a defensive back in 1958. In those days, teams had smaller rosters, and the players often lined up on both the defensive and offensive side of the ball. Jackson was also the Riders third-string quarterback and was only given the opportunity to become the starting QB when both the players ahead of him on the depth chart were injured.

Fortunately for Jackson, Ottawa was a running team, and the rookie quarterback only had to throw the ball about 20 times a game. This gave him the chance to perfect his skills, allowing him to grow into his later role as a dominant offensive player. Since 1969, the year Jackson retired, no Canadian quarterback has been given a meaningful chance to be a starter in the CFL.

Quarterbacks coming out of Canadian universities are not as well trained as their American counterparts, and CFL coaches have been reluctant to give Canadian quarterbacks the time to develop. The league is also dominated by American coaches and general managers who traditionally have had the mindset that American players are the best choice to play quarterback. Canadian quarterbacks were further hamstrung, until 1986, by the "designated import" rule, which allowed teams to dress a third American quarterback without having to drop another imported player.

After Jackson's retirement, Ottawa struggled to find a replacement at the quarterback position. Another Canadian seemed like the perfect candidate. Bill Robinson had guided two different schools to Vanier Cup titles in 1973 and 1974. He was named to the all-Canadian university team at quarterback. Robinson had attended the Ottawa Rough Riders training camp in 1974, but was released.

A league rule allowed Ottawa to keep him on their "protected list" for 1975. Rough Riders fans were hoping Robinson would get a real chance to compete for a job. In the off-season, however, Ottawa had signed two highly touted American prospects—Tom Clements from Notre Dame and Condredge Holloway from the University of Tennessee.

Robinson was the odd man out again.

Even before training camp, Robinson was treated like a second-class prospect: he was sent his $13,000 contract in the mail, none of the money was guaranteed, there was no signing bonus and negotiating the terms of the agreement was not allowed. It was take it or leave it. He was not even invited to the press conference announcing the new quarterback candidates.

At training camp, Robinson was virtually ignored, but his skills seemed to rival those of the two American players. Tony Gabriel, the team's star tight end said, "He's definitely pro status and, in my opinion, the best passer in camp."

During an intra-squad game, Robinson completed 10 of 13 passes. The media and fans began to notice his skills. In the first pre-season game, he completed three of six passes, including a 48-yard reception to Gabriel. Even his QB rival,

Tom Clements, was complimentary: "He's real good, throws a super pass. Better than me. He's got everything as far as I can see."

After his performance, Robinson was only given eight minutes of playing time in the three remaining exhibition games. George Reed, president of the CFL Players' Association blasted Ottawa for its treatment of the young Canadian: "Robinson is the best Canadian college quarterback I've seen since I came up here to play, but it doesn't matter—Ottawa has invested heavily in Americans, and they pretty well have to play them."

The fans also ripped into the Rough Riders, criticizing the team on open-line radio programs and in newspaper editorials. Ottawa, however, had guaranteed the contracts of Clements and Holloway. Robinson was placed on the 21-day injury list with tonsillitis, even though they had been removed years earlier. Coaches told him to work on his defensive-back and special-team skills if he wanted a chance of making the team.

"I'm a quarterback. I've always been one," said a devastated Robinson after the club's decision. "I've played the Canadian game, and the Americans coming up haven't. Why can't I be a quarterback in this league?"

Robinson returned to the roster for a brief time as a spot defensive back and special-teams player. Ottawa cut him, and he later returned to his home in Halifax.

A number of Canadian university quarterbacks have tried to crack the CFL since Jackson's retirement. Western Ontario QB Jamie Bone attended Hamilton's train camp in 1979 but was cut. Bone took the Tiger-Cats before an Ontario Human Rights tribunal, alleging he was never given a fair chance to compete for a job because of his nationality. During the proceedings, the club actually admitted to having made up its mind before camp on who the starters would be, and Bone won the case. The tribunal awarded him $10,000 and ordered the Tiger-Cats to give him a 14-day tryout in 1980. Instead, Bone went south of the border and was cut by the Dallas Cowboys. He never returned to the CFL.

The University of Toronto's Dan Ferady tried out with the Argonauts and made their practice roster in 1981, but opted to return to school. The next year, he was offered the opportunity to try out in the NFL but was cut. For the next two years, he was given brief auditions in the CFL, USFL and NFL.

Bob Cameron came out of Acadia University with the nickname "Acadian Rifle" and was determined to become a quarterback in the CFL. He tried out for every team in the league, but was only offered a job as a kicker. He finally settled in Winnipeg and became the best punter in CFL history, finally retiring at the age of 48.

There were great expectations on Greg Vavra to become the next Russ Jackson after his graduation from the University of Calgary in 1983. Vavra had led the Dinosaurs to a national championship in his final season as the starting quarterback and was named the most valuable player in Canadian college football.

Vavra had also handled the team's place-kicking and punting duties, and it was assumed that when the Calgary Stampeders signed him, he might become a kicker. The Stampeders, however, were not a very good football team. They were in rebuilding mode and having a homegrown quarterback on the field seemed like a great way to draw fans to the stadium while the team struggled. The problem was that the young quarterback wasn't ready to be a starter.

"I was doing games with the CBC then, and we would go in there to cover games, and the media would start on Vavra right away," recalled CFL legend Ron Lancaster in his role as a broadcaster. "They wanted him under centre. Well, finally the coaches put him in, but he simply wasn't ready to be a starter, and when they threw him in the fire I think it kind of destroyed him as a quarterback. He played too soon, and it stunted his career. Lucky for him, he's gone on to success in other fields, but not everyone is so fortunate."

Vavra ended up having a five-year stint in the CFL before retiring as a player in 1988. "With my skill set, I think I got as much out of it as I possibly could have," said the former Stampeder, Eskimo and Lion. "I was a journeyman-type player. I think if a break here or there could have gone my way, I would have played a lot longer than I did. But I had a great experience. I don't have any regrets."

After retiring from the gridiron, Vavra earned a law degree and is now in charge of a small, family-run oil and gas company in Calgary. He is also the offensive co-coordinator of his alma mater, the University of Calgary Dinosaurs, and coaches baseball as well.

Guilo Caravatta, who tried to win a starting QB job in BC during the early 1990s, summed up the perception coaches had about Canadian quarterbacks: "If a rookie from Notre Dame makes a mistake, 'He's learning.' If a Canadian does the same, 'He can't play.'"

In 1991, Caravatta won a job with the Lions when he was clearly the second-best QB behind Doug Flutie. However, when Flutie left BC the next season to play in Calgary, Caravatta knew he would never be able to win the starter's job. In his stint with the team as a backup, 10 quarterbacks (all American) were given the opportunity to start ahead of Caravatta.

In 1996, Acadia produced a quarterback prospect who had the raw skills to be drafted by the NFL. Larry Jusdanis was invited to the NFL Combines to showcase his talents, but a case of nerves resulted in a mediocre performance. He was not even offered a free-agent tryout opportunity.

Most Canadian universities use a simple, run-dominated offence, but Jusdanis had flourished in Acadia where the Axemen employed a "West Coast"-style system. Jusdanis regularly threw over 40 passes a game, catching the eye of scouts from both the CFL and the NFL.

In 2004, the Winnipeg Blue Bombers invited Queen's University quarterback Tommy Dennison for a tryout. He was cut before the first pre-season game. No other team picked him up. Laval's Mathieu Bertrand did win a spot with the Edmonton Eskimos, but only when he switched positions from QB to fullback.

And what about life after football for the league's greatest Canadian quarterback? When the Ottawa Rough Riders drafted Russ Jackson, he negotiated his own contract and made certain it included open plane tickets so he could complete his teaching certificate at the Ontario College of Education. He taught for several years in Ottawa and was principal at two different high schools before coaching the Argos.

In 1977, Jackson returned to the classroom and served as principal at three high schools in the Brampton and Mississauga area. He retired in 1994 as head of John Fraser Secondary School in his hometown of Hamilton. He maintained a connection to the league by doing some promotional work for the Canadian Football Hall of Fame and the Canadian Sports Hall of Fame, as well as doing radio broadcasts for the Tiger-Cats for five seasons.

The Canadian quarterback debate has continued for decades. Canadians have traditionally found themselves slotted into certain positions—kickers, fullbacks, offensive linemen, slotbacks or safeties. The other "skilled positions" have been reserved for American imports. Fortunately this convention has begun to erode—all eight CFL rosters now have at least a handful of Canadians in such positions as wide receiver, linebacker,

running back, defensive lineman and cornerback. In 2008, however, not one Canadian quarterback was listed on the roster of any CFL club.

Grandpa Allen

Damon Allen became more efficient as
a quarterback when he reached his 40s than he
was when he broke into the league over 20 years
earlier. Allen was blessed with talent, ability
and durability. No quarterback has thrown for
more yards—72,381, shattering the record that
had previously been held by Warren Moon, who
played six seasons in the CFL and 17 more in
the NFL.

Allan came out of Cal State–Fullerton as
a passing quarterback, where he set an NCAA
record for attempting 329 consecutive passes with
just one interception. He dreamed of playing in
the NFL, but he was a stick figure at 6'1" and 157
pounds. Allen turned pro in 1985, the same year
his older brother Marcus was starring as a running back with the Super Bowl XVIII–winning
Los Angeles Raiders.

Damon Allen didn't receive a legitimate offer
to quarterback in the United States, although pro
teams did call to see if he was interested in

playing wide receiver or defensive back. Instead, Allen held on to his dream and headed north to play for the Edmonton Eskimos. Later he recalled that in his first year with the Eskimos his teammates voted him "most likely to freeze to death, because I was from California."

Instead it was the start of a 23-year career with seven CFL teams—Edmonton, Ottawa, Hamilton, Edmonton again, Memphis, BC and Toronto. Along the journey, he developed from a running, athletic, Michael Vick–type QB—he holds the CFL record for rushing yards by a quarterback with 11,920—to a methodical passer.

"I've always been a Damon Allen fan," explained Don Matthews, the league's all-time leading coach in career wins, "but he's gained maturity as a passer in recent years. He's reading defences, dumping the ball off, showing great patience. He's become a more sophisticated quarterback."

In 2003, after seven seasons with the Lions, Allen became expendable and was snapped up by the Argos.

"He may be approaching 40, but physically he's a lot younger than that," said Toronto general manager Adam Rita at the time. "I think he's still got a Grey Cup left in him."

Rita was right. In 2004, at the age of 41and the grandfather of a two-and-a-half-year-old boy, Allen led the Toronto Argonauts to a first-place finish and a 27–19 Grey Cup victory over BC. He was named the game's most outstanding player. The Throwin' Grandpa had passed for 299 yards and a touchdown, and rushed for two others in the upset win. It was his fourth Grey Cup—in two of those victories he was named the game's MVP.

"There isn't a long list of quarterbacks in their 40s, but with athletes taking better care of their bodies and with technology, guys are playing longer," explained Allen after the season. "And it's not like I'm hanging on. Teams have wanted me. In a way, that's humbling."

The next season, the Argos finished in first place again, but stumbled in the Eastern final against Montréal. Allen had his best season ever and won the CFL's Most Outstanding Player award for the first time in his long career.

The end finally neared in 2007, when he lost his starting quarterback job to Michael Bishop. When Bishop faltered, Allen again became the starter, but went down soon after with a season-ending toe injury. In the off-season, the Argos obtained Kerry Joseph, who was coming off the CFL's Outstanding Player award and the

Grey Cup game MVP, from the Saskatchewan Roughriders. It was time for Allen to leave the game as a player.

Sometimes in the world of sports "ageless" is thrown around too much, but when Damon Allen retired in 2008 at 44, he left the game unscathed. In fact, he looked like he could still be a starting QB in the league. After 23 seasons of professional football, Allen was asked to name his greatest accomplishment. He answered with one word, "durability."

Chapter Six

Importing Trouble

Over the years, many American imports have crossed the border to play in the CFL. For players such as Warren Moon and Joe Theismann, their years in Canada served as an apprenticeship before they became impact performers in the NFL.

The success that Doug Flutie and Joe Kapp enjoyed in Canadian football allowed them to return to the United States to resume careers that had previously bogged down in their native land. Rocket Ismail and Tom Cousineau were lured to the land of ice and snow by the offer of big bucks.

And then there were the troublemakers. Over the years, the CFL has become a haven for players who have found themselves without a football home south of the 49th parallel. For many, the CFL was not the land of redemption, just another brief stop in their journey out of football.

Johnny Rodgers

In 1972, the great college running back Johnny Rodgers signed with the Montréal Alouettes. The Heisman Trophy winner had led Nebraska to a pair of national titles and a 32–2–2 record as the team's starting tailback. But Rodgers had also been one of three men found guilty of robbing a Lincoln, Nebraska, gas station attendant of $91 in 1970. The 19-year-old freshman was sentenced to probation and was allowed to continue attending college and playing football.

The Alouettes were looking for a big name to help fill the newly completed Olympic Stadium and to compete with the Argos, who had signed big-name college players like Joe Theismann and Leon McQuay. Despite Rodgers' criminal record, Montréal offered the star runner over $100,000 per season, topping the NFL. Rodgers bolted north of the border.

In his last season playing for Nebraska, Rodgers had been in more trouble with the law. He pled guilty to driving with a suspended licence and running a stop sign. After playing in the

Orange Bowl, Rodgers was ordered to serve his 30-day sentence in a local prison. While in jail, Alouettes general manager J.I. Albrecht had called him every day to sell the young star on coming to Canada.

Rodgers was an immediate CFL star and helped define a new position—wingback. He lined up as a running back, but his primary role was to catch the football. In his rookie season in 1973, he caught 41 catches for 841 yards and added another 303 rushing yards on 55 carries. The next season he was even better, hauling in 60 catches for 1024 yards, while increasing his rushing total to 402 yards on 87 carries.

In 1975, the CFL allowed blocking on punts for the first time. Up to then, talented runners were not used to return punts because the coverage teams were allowed uncontested hits on the poor sod fielding the punt. Rodgers was already an accomplished kickoff returner, but the rule change allowed him to excel as a punt returner. In 1975, the former Husker returned 60 punts for 912 yards, including a 101-yard touchdown. The next season, his punt returns totalled 931 yards. Thrown in with his receiving and rushing totals, Rodgers was the dominant offensive force in the league.

Rodgers played for the Als from 1973 to 1976, helping them to win a Grey Cup. He left the CFL the following season to become a wide receiver with the San Diego Chargers. Montréal coach Marv Levy was happy to see Rodgers head south, though. After the Alouettes lost the Eastern final 23–0 to Toronto, it was leaked to the media that Rodgers had missed an important team meeting the evening before the game.

The *Toronto Star* printed a scathing editorial on Rodgers' behaviour:

> *Rodgers will pay a fine for playing hooky as he has done before when he as missed workouts or arrived late, but the punishment is meaningless to him...nothing more than a mildly irritating effect of doing what he pleases while the ranks and file of his teammates, fellows who can't afford $1000 for an evening of fun are required to obey the rules... Levy has made a serious mistake in allowing Rodgers to flout club rules. The cost of the blunder has been immense—the disintegration of an excellent club.*

With the Chargers, Rodgers suffered hamstring problems in his first year, severely limiting his effectiveness. He then suffered a career-ending foot injury when a teammate stepped on him during his second Chargers training camp. By 1980, he was out of football.

In 1987, Rodgers had another run-in with the law when he was convicted of assault and illegal gun possession for an incident involving a cable television repairman who was disconnecting service to his San Diego home. The assault conviction was reversed on appeal, but Rodgers served three years' probation for the gun charge.

To his credit, Rodgers bounced back to start his own business, Jet Wear Inc., which markets and distributes NCAA collegiate-licenced juvenile bedding products. He also was a partner in an Omaha sports bar, a venture that was complicated by his conviction in the gas station holdup. As a convicted felon, Nebraska law prohibited him from holding a liquor licence.

At the same time that Rodgers was receiving all-star accolades in Montréal, the league sent out a message that proper behaviour was required from its players. Winnipeg released two of its outstanding receivers, Mark Herron (a runner-up for league MVP in 1972) and Jim Thorpe after they were charged with illegal possession of marijuana and cocaine. Hamilton also waived all-American Steve Wooster from their roster after he was convicted of a dope charge. The league seemed to be sending out mixed messages when Rodgers, a convicted felon, was allowed to play.

Ricky Williams

In recent years, the CFL has served as a rehab centre for NFL drug offenders. The league has no drug policy at all, making it a refuge for NFL players who have been suspended. The most famous American import to sharpen his football skills while on suspension was Ricky Williams.

In 2006, the Toronto Argonauts signed the all-pro running back to a $240,000 contract. Williams had been suspended for a year after failing his fourth drug test (the first three for marijuana; the fourth for an undisclosed substance). In 2004, Williams had walked away from the game after failing his third test. The Miami Dolphins claimed the former Heisman Trophy winner owed the team $5.4 million for not fulfilling the terms of his contract.

His premature retirement had been well publicized, and during the few months he was away from football, Williams had become a New-Age hippie, moving to the Australian outback, camping and looking for God. He took up yoga, earning a teaching certificate in India. The vegetarian with the thick beard and dreadlocks was football's version of Bob Marley.

The signing of Williams helped the Argos fill the SkyDome, and number 27 jerseys were snapped up by Toronto fans. On the field, the 5'10", 220-pound running back showed bursts of the skill and power that had made him one of the elite players in the NFL. The rustiness also showed. The Argos themselves were an inconsistent bunch. Without the support of a skilled offensive line, Williams was a non-factor in many of the games he played in. The 29-year-old also struggled with injuries for much of the year.

In allowing Williams to play in the CFL, Miami had secured a written promise from the Argos that their star property would go back to the Dolphins in 2007. Williams was under great pressure to return—a court had ruled that the running back owed Miami two seasons' worth of salary. To be considered for reinstatement in the NFL, Williams was drug tested up to 10 times per month and stayed clean while in Canada. In his 11-game stay with the Argos, Williams rushed for 526 yards and two touchdowns and caught 19 passes for 127 yards.

Before heading south after the 2006 season, Williams had only good things to say about his stay with the Argos. "It's easier for me to be a person up here," he said in parting. "Since it's not so much of a business, I'm not so much of a product. If you value money, it's better to be in the NFL. If you value life, it's better up here."

Williams was reinstated by the NFL in November 2007 and returned to the Dolphins. The 2002 NFL rushing leader has managed to stay clean, but the temptation to turn to marijuana is always lurking. He battles the urge to smoke pot by meditating.

Another positive drug test would likely end Williams' football career. "I have no space, no wiggle room," admits the eight-year veteran.

The Gangster League

In classic Westerns, desperados and bandits often fled the law by heading south to Mexico in a bid to escape the jurisdiction of the sheriffs and marshals who were tracking them. In the NFL, bad dudes looking for a second chance to revive their football careers head north to Canada to play in the CFL.

"We're like many other employers that do not discriminate for criminal offences," explained Michael Copeland, the league's chief operating officer in 2006. "If you have a criminal record, you're entitled to seek employment."

Andre Rison was one of the NFL's best receivers before he was suspended for four games for violating the league's substance-abuse policy. The former Pro Bowler continued a downward slide, which led to his departure from football. In a last-gasp attempt to get back into the game, Rison spent parts of two CFL seasons with the Toronto Argonauts, where he only caught 14 passes for 174 yards and one touchdown.

Lawrence Phillips was a star running back at the University of Nevada who, even in college, led a troubled life away from the gridiron. In 1996, the Husker star pled no contest to misdemeanour trespassing and assault after he beat and kicked his girlfriend, pulled her down three flights of stairs by the hair and slammed her head into a wall.

After being selected sixth overall in the 1996 NFL draft, he rubbed three teams the wrong way. Miami cut him after he was charged with striking a woman in the face at a nightclub (again he pled no contest). He was arrested for impaired driving in St. Louis and had a confrontation with police in Omaha. In Los Angeles, he pled no contest to allegations that he beat a woman.

Despite his on-field talent, no other NFL team was willing to take a chance on Phillips. So north he came, finding a home in Montréal. Coach Don Matthews publicly supported the running back's comeback, and Phillips responded by rushing for 1022 yards and 13 TDs. Off the field, Phillips couldn't stay out of trouble, though. The Alouettes released him after the 2002 season when he was charged with sexually assaulting his girlfriend. The next fall, Calgary cut him after he argued with coach Jim Barker.

In August 2005, the 33-year-old former Cornhusker star was jailed when he drove onto a field near Los Angeles Memorial Coliseum and struck three boys, ages 14 and 15, and a 19-year-old man with his car. All three suffered cuts and bruises. The car narrowly missed three other people. Phillips was allegedly upset after losing a pickup football game to the youths and accused them of stealing some of his possessions. He was convicted of seven counts of assault with a deadly weapon. The sentencing was delayed for two years, but in October 2008, he received a 10-year prison term.

In 2005, the Ottawa Renegades added Dimitrius Underwood to their roster. The former first-round draft pick of the Minnesota Vikings in 1999 suffered from bipolar disorder. He only played 19 games in three NFL seasons and was forced out of professional football in 2001.

Underwood was in and out of mental-health institutions on at least three occasions. The defensive lineman suffered violent mood swings and attempted suicide twice in public. He was also convicted twice for assaulting a police officer (for which he was sentenced to five years' probation) and even robbed someone who was confined to a wheelchair.

In 2004, he was taken to a psychiatric ward in a Dallas hospital after an incident during which police doused him with pepper spray. Underwood had stalled his vehicle on a freeway and, when approached by police, he told the officers he wasn't coming out. Police had to block the freeway, shatter a window and pelt the former Cowboy with pepper-spray balls fired from a special gun.

Four years after Underwood's last NFL game, Ottawa decided to take a chance on the troubled defender. Renegades general manager and coach, Joe Paopao, stated that everyone deserved a second chance and vowed to keep a close watch on the 28-year-old. Unfortunately, this confidence turned out to be misplaced, and Underwood was released after only a few games.

In 2006, the Hamilton Tiger-Cats signed Anthony Davis, who in 2003 had pled guilty to punching his girlfriend in the face. Prosecutors later dropped the case after Davis took part in a first-offenders program. In the same season, Kyries Hebert was added to Winnipeg's practice roster even though he had pled guilty to two misdemeanours in connection to a domestic dispute. The police arrested him, though he was never charged, for allegedly holding his wife's head under water and threatening to kill her in a fight over an unpaid cell-phone bill.

In another high-profile case that rocked Saskatchewan, Roughrider Trevis Smith was found guilty of two counts of aggravated assault for having unprotected sex with two women without telling them he was HIV positive. He was suspended immediately, but the league suffered an embarrassing blow to its image.

Minnesota Vikings running back Onterrio Smith garnered headlines across North America in May 2005 when he was caught at the Minneapolis-St. Paul airport with dried urine and a "Whizzinater," a device used to beat drug tests. The man that Winnipeg fans would nickname the Blue Bonger had failed four drug tests for having marijuana in his system. Smith was suspended for the 2005 season, and, after spending seven months in rehab, the 25-year-old was signed in May 2006 by the Winnipeg Blue Bombers, even though he was facing a civil suit in Minneapolis related to a sexual assault case. Overweight and out of shape, he was cut a month later.

Besides signing Ricky Williams, the Toronto Argonauts have led the CFL in American reclamation projects. In the 2006 season alone, the Argos' roster included offensive tackle Bernard Williams, a first-round NFL pick in 1994 who had been busted a couple of times by the league for marijuana use; R. Jay Soward, a receiver who battled alcoholism and was suspended by the NFL in 2002 for repeatedly breaking the league's substance-abuse policy; and wideout Robert Baker who spent 10 months in prison for trafficking cocaine.

Dexter Manley

In his prime, Dexter Manley was the most feared pass rusher in the NFL—a 6'5", 260-pound projectile who terrorized quarterbacks for 10 seasons. By 1991, though, he had failed more drug tests (four) than he had Super Bowl rings (three) and was banned for life.

Two years later, Manley was give another chance when the Ottawa Renegades signed him for his star power. He was no longer a dominant player, and the signing was viewed by many in the media as a publicity stunt to generate some excitement for a franchise that was hopelessly unsuccessful.

The Washington Redskins had drafted Manley in the fifth round, and he worked his way up the football ladder, first as a special-teams player, then gaining a spot on the defensive line before developing into the team's featured pass rusher. He had several colourful incidents off the field during his early years in the NFL. He was busted by a SWAT team for impersonating an officer, and he trashed hotel rooms and the odd locker room.

"I said I was going to raise hell on the field and off," he told reporters at the time. "And I haven't let anyone down yet. I don't have a problem with booze, I have a problem with living."

Manley was not only a drinker; he discovered cocaine in 1981, his rookie year. In the days leading up to the 1988 Super Bowl, he claimed that the Redskins covered up a failed drug test so he could play in the big game. He was so hooked on the drug that he actually searched the locker room on his hands and knees for a missing coke spoon while coach Joe Gibbs watched.

After his third Super Bowl, Manley was near the top of the salary scale, earning $600,000 per season and blowing much of it on cocaine. He was caught three times through drug testing and received a lifetime ban from the league in 1989. That expulsion lasted only 13 months, then he was reinstated by the NFL and signed a contract with the Arizona Cardinals. In 1991, however, he failed his fourth drug test and was banned for life, this time for good.

In 1993, Lonie Glieberman, who left a legacy of killing CFL franchises, decided that his Ottawa Renegades should be a halfway house for multiple violators of the NFL's substance-abuse policy. Manley was signed to a one-year contract, but his best days as a player were over. He was too slow for the wide-open Canadian game.

When the Manley signing was announced, several Renegades were less than thrilled. "This has taken the Renegades down to the level of professional wrestling...not only is Lonie insulting the players in this dressing room, he's insulting the football fans of Ottawa who want honest-to-goodness football, not cheap marketing crap," grumbled Ottawa centre Irv Daymond.

"Why do we take pay cuts when [the Glieber-mans] have that kind of money to throw around?" asked linebacker Greg Stuman. "It's a slap in the face to every player in that room. He's not going to help."

Manley only lasted 16 plays in his first game in an Ottawa uniform. He suffered a hyperextended elbow and a slight tear in his knee. Some of his Renegade teammates publicly questioned the injuries, claiming that Manley was physically able to play.

Despite having only a 3–14 record, Ottawa still could qualify for the playoffs by defeating Hamilton in their last regular season game. Late in the fourth quarter, Manley hit Tiger-Cat quarterback Todd Dillon, forcing a fumble. Ottawa recovered and scored the winning touchdown in a 27–26 victory. These were Manley's first statistics in the CFL—a tackle and a fumble recovery.

Unexpectedly, the big defensive lineman was in the news for his actions on the field. Manley took advantage of his new-found credibility, promising to sack Dillon three more times and cause at least two fumble recoveries against Hamilton in their playoff semifinal the next week. But Manley was fined for revealing that the team had offered a pre-game reward for any player who could knock Dillon out of the game.

In the Eastern semifinal, Hamilton defeated Ottawa 21–10. Manley had no sacks, no fumble recoveries and no tackles. It was his last game in the league. His addiction to drugs resurfaced after his release from the CFL. Over the next decade. he would be in and out of jail for cocaine possession.

Chapter Seven

Great Plays

As the old cliché goes, "Football is won in the trenches." It's a truism that invokes an unmistakable image: big men—offensive and defensive linemen—hammering away at each other, looking for that slight advantage on the line of scrimmage to allow the running back to slip through a seam or to clear a path for a blitzing linebacker to drop the quarterback. And while this may be true over the grind of a 60-minute game, over an 18-game season, over one or two playoff games leading up to the Grey Cup, it is often the unexpected—a fake punt, a quarterback sneak or an option pass from the tailback—that provides the spark required for victory.

At the 1973 Grey Cup, Tom Wilkinson, the wily quarterback from the Edmonton Eskimos, had the Ottawa Rough Riders freaked out before the ball was even snapped. The chunky QB with the droopy pants was continually accused of using "an unnatural head motion to draw the defence offside."

Frank Clair, the Ottawa general manager, lobbied loud and often to league officials to watch Wilkinson carefully on the line of scrimmage: "I'm not saying that Edmonton designs the play for Wilkinson, but when we, Ottawa, went up against them, we went offside five times just because of him, and normally we don't go offside."

Wilkinson's deceptive head fake was never a factor in the Cup classic. A couple of Ottawa's big defenders broke his ribs early in the game, and the Rough Riders prevailed 22–18. It was clear decision favouring brute force over trickery. On other occasions, however, deception has triumphed.

Electronic eavesdropping was a hot topic in the league during the 1994 season. Adam Rita, the coach of the Ottawa Rough Riders, had allowed the ESPN2 broadcast team to wire him up with a live microphone during a game against Winnipeg. The idea was to inform American viewers of the plays being sent in from the sidelines (at the time, ESPN2 was not available in Canada).

As luck would have it, the Blue Bombers' director of player personnel, Paul Jones, happened to be in Tennessee while on a scouting assignment and tuned into the broadcast. When he realized he could hear Rita calling plays, he phoned Bombers' assistant general manager Lyle Bauer in the Winnipeg Stadium press box. Bauer relayed the information to Winnipeg coach Cal Murphy, who in turn called a defence to stop the play. The Blue Bombers won 46–1.

It was the last time a coach in the CFL agreed to be miked for a live telecast.

The Catch

The 1976 Grey Cup at Toronto's Exhibition Stadium featured one of the most heart-grabbing climaxes in the long history of the championship game. In all the history of the wide-open, pass-happy CFL, it is remembered as "The Catch."

Some 54,000 fans showed up to witness the Saskatchewan Roughriders led by the Little General, quarterback Ron Lancaster, and the league's all-time leading rusher, George Reed, take on the underdog Ottawa Rough Riders. The Roughriders were seven-point favourites and, late in the fourth quarter, held a 20–16 advantage.

In the final minute, Saskatchewan was forced to punt into a strong wind. Ottawa was given great field position at the Roughriders 35-yard line. With only 44 seconds left to play, Tom Clements, the second-year Ottawa quarterback, had a final opportunity to get the ball in the end zone. Tony Gabriel, the outstanding Canadian tight end, caught Clements' pass at the Saskatchewan 20. In the pileup that followed the tackle, Gabriel took a shot on the back of neck. The late hit didn't knock the all-star out, but he emerged from the pile in a dazed state. In the huddle for the next play, a teammate noticed the confusion in Gabriel's eyes and urged him to concentrate, telling him, "Come on, Gabe. Time's running out."

A play came in from the sidelines, but Clements ignored the coach's preference and called, "Rob I, fake 34, tight-end flag." In his book, *Double Trouble*, Gabriel explained how the final play unfolded:

> *In the Ottawa huddle when Clements calls a play, he uses a kind of shorthand. In our huddles, "Rob" instructs the tight end to line up on the right side of the line. The "I" indicates the backfield formation—halfback and*

fullback lined up directly behind each other and the quarterback. The whole "30-series" of plays refers to running plays with the number 3 back, the fullback, the third man in the "I," carrying the ball. The "4" in the "34" means the fullback, will hit the number 4 hole, the space between the right guard and the tackle. Naturally enough, the "fake" means what it says—it's made to look like a running play to dupe the opposition.

Now, having established all that information, Tommy then says "tight-end flag," which means he wants the tight end, on the right side of the line, to head downfield and cut to the flag. The flag is the pennant mounted on the flexible metal stand, which marks each end of both goal lines. That's the play Tom called.

For a second or so the players on the line and in the backfield blocked as if for a run; the number 3 back moved as if to take a handoff from Clements. Then, the tight end broke downfield, put a couple of moves on some defenders, and well inside the Saskatchewan end zone, pulled in the pass. Touchdown. Game. The Grey Cup. I was that tight end.

A week earlier, in the Eastern final against Hamilton, Clements had called the same play and delivered the ball perfectly to Gabriel in the corner of the end zone. The tight end, however, lost his concentration when a defender waved at the ball, and the pigskin slipped off his fingers. Fortunately, Ottawa was ahead 14–0 at the time and held on for a 17–15 victory.

Relief then, was the initial emotion Gabriel felt when he hauled in the pass and clinched the Grey Cup. As Clements released the ball, Gabriel remembered thinking, "Let nothing distract me," and as he pulled it in, "I proved I could do it."

Teammate Gary Kuzyk, who was downfield with Gabriel on the play, remembered the look on his teammate's face as he prepared to catch the ball: "His eyes were six feet wide open." The pro-Eastern crowd erupted with the touchdown. Ontario Premier William Davis had to fight his way through the stands to join Prime Minister Pierre Trudeau and CFL Commissioner Jake Gaudaur at midfield to present the trophy to the winning team.

In the ensuing days, both Clements and Gabriel were asked to relive the game and the pass during countless interview requests. The Canadian tight end became known as "the guy that won the Grey Cup." Gabriel always felt uncomfortable with the notion that the contribution of any one individual was greater than the efforts of the team. When asked to sign an autograph in the days after the victory, he penned: "With best wishes from all the Riders and especially from Tony Gabriel."

Big Ange Knocks Out Willie Fleming

In the CFL's long history, only a few players have transcended the game to gain celebrity status. On of them was Angelo Mosca, whose thick, dark hair, fierce eyes and scowling mouth became instantly recognizable across Canada.

For the 15 years he played professional football, right up to his retirement in 1972, the huge 6'4", 275-pound lineman terrorized his opponents. "Big Ange" had a mean reputation that he enthusiastically fostered with his actions and words.

"I have nothing against clean play, but what's a clean shoestring tackle got that an elbow smash to the head hasn't?" he growled during one interview.

Mosca survived a bumpy start on his journey to the CFL. After an American college career that included getting kicked out of Notre Dame for bookmaking on football games and another ejection from the University of Wyoming for stealing typewriters and cameras at local stores and then selling them on campus, Mosca was drafted by the Philadelphia Eagles.

He was offered more money to play in Canada, so he came north, but he bounced from team to team after rubbing his coaches in Hamilton, Ottawa and Montréal the wrong way. Mosca finally realized he might be the problem and asked the Tiger-Cats for another audition. He became a fixture with the Ticats, playing in nine Grey Cups and winning five championships. He was also a six-time all-star.

Mosca cemented his reputation as a tough guy during the 1963 Grey Cup in Vancouver. The Tiger-Cats were up against the hometown BC Lions, who were led offensively by halfback Willie Fleming and quarterback Joe Kapp. Late in the second quarter, Fleming took a pass from Kapp and started around the end towards the sideline. The running back was hit by a Ticats defender and fell forward to the ground. Big Ange had been running hard to the sideline and hurled himself through the air to cut Fleming off just as the running back hit the turf. Mosca landed on top of the Lions star.

"That made my career," said Mosca. "I'll never forget the hit. He was running near the sidelines. Joe Zuger came up to get him, and I pursued him laterally. I dove after him, and my knee hit him in the helmet. He was knocked out of the game. People thought it was a cheap shot, but it really wasn't."

Fleming had been knocked out cold and never returned to the game. Kapp was incensed, as was the Vancouver crowd. Mosca was penalized on the play, but without their dynamic halfback, the Lions lost 21–10. The Mosca-Fleming incident made headlines across Canada as football fans debated whether it was a great play or a late hit.

"I knew that by people thinking I was dirty, it would help me personally," recalled the Ticat lineman years later. "I wound up doing all kinds of commercials and endorsements."

The legend of Mosca continued to grow after a number of off-field escapades. In one incident he drove a car through the front window of a downtown Hamilton restaurant. When the manager of the place approached him, he asked for a beer to go. During one off-season, he had to be pulled off an official after disagreeing with a call in a summer basketball league. He punched out a doorman out at a bar and decked all comers in a nightclub brawl.

Before the 1967 Grey Cup in Ottawa, Mosca and the Ticats had just completed a practice and were walking to the parking lot when an Ottawa player named Jerry Seliger showed up. Mosca and Seliger did not like each other. The Ottawa player called him a name. Big Ange turned, walked over to him, knocked him cold with one punch, stepped over him and headed to the team bus.

"The only reason that Angelo ever got into trouble with people was because when you're that big and you're an athlete and you have notoriety, everyone wants to take a shot at you, verbally and otherwise," summed up a teammate.

In 1960, Mosca began moonlighting as a professional wrestler. His reputation as a football player cast him perfectly to fit the villain role; he was dubbed "King Kong" and commanded big fees on the wrestling circuit. After he retired from football in 1972, Mosca wrestled for another decade, earning up to $50,000 per season.

Trick Plays

In the 1948 Grey Cup, the Calgary Stampeders pulled off a version of the "sleeper play" that proved pivotal in their 12–7 victory over Ottawa. With the Stampeders trailing, Calgary fans received more bad news when halfback Normie

Hill appeared to be injured. As he lay on the turf, quarterback Keith Spaith called the next play in the huddle. As the teams lined up, Ottawa ignored Hill, who was still flopping around on the field. Spaith took the snap; Hill miraculously got to his feet and began running down the side- lines. The Rough Riders had nobody assigned to the running back, and Spaith hit him perfectly with the pass. Hill ran into the end zone, giving the Stampeders a lead that they never gave up. The "sleeper play" was finally banned in 1961.

In the 1978 Grey Cup, on a third down, the Edmonton Eskimos lined up for a field goal at the Montréal Alouette 15-yard line. It would be an almost automatic three points for the great Eskimo kicker Dave Cutler. As usual, the ball went from Edmonton centre Bob Howes to quar- terback Tom Wilkinson. But instead of placing the ball for Cutler's field-goal attempt, Wilkinson flipped the pigskin to receiver Tom Scott, who was already moving down the field.

Edmonton gained the necessary yardage for the first down. Two plays later, the Eskimos scored the touchdown and would eventually win the Grey Cup 20–13. After the game, Edmonton head coach Hugh Campbell was asked how much the team had rehearsed the trick play.

"We ran it once during the open practice this week, when you guys [the reporters] had moved to the other side of the field," replied Campbell. "You have to use creative thinking when you're a head coach, and I have quite an imagination," he added. After a brief pause, Campbell smiled and confessed, "Actually, I saw it on the halftime highlights on Monday Night Football. I think the Seahawks used it."

The Weirdest Play in Football

In 1961, the Toronto Argonauts and Hamilton Tiger-Cats met in a two-game, total-points Eastern final. Led by quarterback Tobin Rote (from the Detroit Lions and Green Bay Packers), the Argos whipped the Tiger-Cats 25–7 in the first game, taking an 18-point advantage into Hamilton for game two.

The Tiger-Cats dominated at Ivor Wynne Stadium, holding Toronto's offence to two points while piling up 20 of their own to tie the total two-game score 27–27. In the final minute, Toronto's Stan Wallace intercepted a pass at the Hamilton 35-yard line. To win the game, all the Argos had to do was score a single point, and with Dave Mann, the best kicker in the game, observers thought Toronto would punt the ball through the Hamilton end zone to move on to the Grey Cup.

Instead, the Argos decided to run the clock down before trying the kick. On the first running play, Toronto was offside, and the ball was moved back to the 40. On the next two plays, the Argos were stuffed at the line of scrimmage. On came Mann to punt the ball.

Don Sutherin, Hamilton's all-star defensive back and the team's kicker, and quarterback Bernie Faloney were sent on to the field to kick Mann's punt out of the end zone. "I caught it 18 yards deep and booted it back," recalled Sutherin. "Mann caught it and kicked it back in. Bernie caught Mann's next punt and returned it 120 yards for a touchdown."

But the game wasn't over. While Faloney was running for a touchdown, various Hamilton players were penalized for illegally blocking the Toronto tacklers. The officials ruled no touchdown, and since time had run out (in those days the game could end on a penalty), the series was still tied.

In overtime, the Tiger-Cats ended up putting their Eastern rivals away, scoring four unanswered touchdowns in a 48–2 victory.

Improvising A Grey Cup Win

In his 25 seasons in the CFL (all with the BC Lions), Lui Passaglia earned a reputation for making big plays in the biggest of games. When he retired from the league in 2000, he was the all-time professional football leader in games played (408), field goals (875), points (3991) and punting yards (133,826). In addition, he holds the CFL record for singles (309), converts (1045) and consecutive converts made (560).

In the 1985 Grey Cup against the Hamilton Tiger-Cats, Passaglia showed his exceptional football instincts for turning near disaster into the turning point of a championship game. Just before halftime, the Lions were trailing 14–13. The Leos' offence had stalled once again, and Passaglia came onto the field to punt.

Hamilton's Mitchell Price broke through the wall in front of the BC kicker just as Passaglia was going to boot the ball. Instead of panicking, the East Vancouver native pulled the ball down, shifted neatly around the on-rushing Price and scampered 12 yards for a BC first down. On the next play, BC quarterback Roy Dewalt found Ned Armour with a touchdown pass. The Lions never gave up the lead, winning the game 37–24.

"Really, I had no choice but to do something because when I was ready to drop the ball I could see yellow and black jerseys—in fact, two of them—coming up the middle," recalled Passaglia. "If I had kicked, it they would have blocked it."

Ticat defensive back Less Browne was one of the Hamilton special-team players that came charging in at Passaglia: "He just took off and ran right up the middle, right past Mitch Price, who had his fingertips on him. That's when they say it's a game of inches. Mitch had his fingertips, I would swear, right on Passaglia's jersey. I kept thinking, 'Just grab him, Mitch, just grab him!' He couldn't, and BC ended up getting that first down, which kept their drive alive."

"There is no doubt that Passaglia changed the momentum of the game with that play," said Tiger-Cats coach Al Bruno. "On that one play he could have been the player of the game... He made one helluva move to get out of there."

Lions coach Don Matthews agreed: "That play saved us...It took the momentum away from Hamilton."

Passaglia was born in 1954, the year of the Lions' first season in the CFL, in a small house six blocks away from Empire Stadium, the original home of the team. He was a receiver at Simon Fraser University and, in 1976, was drafted by BC in the first round of the college draft. In his first regular-season game, a 32–6 loss to Saskatchewan at Empire Stadium, he caught a 10-yard touchdown pass. Little did he know that it would be the last catch of his football career—though he would run for a second touchdown in his last regular-season game in November 2000.

Through the exhibition season, the Lions had tried out six kickers, including future Detroit Lions all-pro Eddie Murray. At the start of the regular season, the club finally decided that the East Vancouver rookie would be their kicker. BC coach Cal Murphy put his job on the line by going with a first-year kicker and punter.

"I was hoping he would last long enough that I could repay him because I was probably so-so at best my first year," recalled the kicker, who only hit 28 out of 49 field-goal attempts and registered a sub-par 41.4-yard punting average in his rookie season.

No one dreamed at the time that Passaglia would hold the job for the next quarter century. The BC Lions were mostly terrible during the 1970s, and, as a string of general managers and coaches passed through the city, younger kickers would be brought into town to challenge for Passaglia's job. He always ended up on top.

Another career highlight came in 1994 when he kicked a game-winning 38-yard field goal against Baltimore to win the Grey Cup. The team from Baltimore represented an American invasion, and there was great pressure on the Lions to stop the Cup from moving south of the border for the first time in its long history. "We were a mixed bag of Canadians and Americans," recalled Passaglia, who was serenaded by BC fans with "Loo, Loo" before each kick. "We were huge underdogs—a 9–9 team with no business being there. The people of Canada wanted it so badly."

Over the years, Passaglia has had to supplement his CFL salary with other jobs to make ends meet. He's worked as a teacher, in his family's construction business, as an insurance agent and in event marketing. At the age of 46, he decided it was time to step away from the playing field. The Lions were on shaky ground at the time; they had become a mediocre team averaging only 22,000 fans in cavernous BC Place Stadium.

In 2000, his last season, Passaglia set a league record by connecting on 40 of 44 field-goal attempts (90.9 percent). And to top off his amazing career, the moustachioed kicker had a chance to go out on top as the Lions advanced to the Grey Cup for the fifth time in his tenure with the team. With 1:25 left on the clock, Passaglia kicked a 29-yard field goal to provide the winning edge as BC defeated the Montréal Alouettes. It was his third Grey Cup victory.

Lui Passaglia knew it was time to retire when his back became sore while standing on the BC Lions sidelines. "You know you're getting old when you're in pain just from standing too long," recalled the legendary Lions kicker. "You're a football player—that's not supposed to happen."

The Greatest Grey Cup Play of All Time

Henry "Gizmo" Williams revolutionized special-teams play, becoming as reliable a scoring weapon as any wide receiver or running back on the Edmonton Eskimos, the team he played for during his entire 14-year career in the CFL.

He was only a barrel-chested 5'6" and 183 pounds, but he was blessed with blazing speed, agility and the uncanny ability to make tacklers miss. He had muscles on top of muscles, allowing him to survive the kamikaze world of kick returning.

The career numbers for Gizmo are astounding. He totalled 23,927 combined yards, including rushing, receiving and kick-return yards on punts, kickoffs and missed field goals. He was such a force that he became the first CFL kick-return specialist; the Eskimos reserved a roster spot to accommodate his skills. He repaid the Edmonton organization by returning 1003 punts for 11,177 yards and 26 touchdowns (the second-best total is 11) and returned 335 kickoffs for 7354 yards and two touchdowns. He had another 28 kick-return touchdowns called back because of penalties.

He also added 1612 yards and three touchdowns on 58 missed field-goal returns. Even though he was never a regular starter on offence, Williams retired ranking 11th best on the Eskimos' all-time receiving yardage with 3644 yards and added another 21 touchdowns. He desperately wanted a 1000-yard season as a receiver and came close in 1993 when he caught 52 passes for 950 yards.

"Before he came, a punt-return touchdown used to be like a hurricane—you might have one this season, you may have three this season, and you may not have one for another five seasons," said Michael "Pinball" Clemons, the great Toronto Argonaut kick returner who followed Gizmo. "He also kept people from getting up, going to get a drink or a snack at that time. They actually made sure they were sitting down when the punt happened so they could watch him."

It was a long, rough journey for Gizmo to become a CFL legend. He grew up in Memphis, Tennessee, and was only six when his mother died of multiple sclerosis. The following year, his father perished in a house fire. Williams ended up living with an older brother and then with an aunt. And there were further family tragedies: a sister died of a drug overdose; MS claimed three other family members; and another brother was fatally shot.

Williams was a kick-returning star in college, leading the NCAA in return yardage in two successive seasons. His short stature kept him out of the NFL, but he found a home with the Memphis Showboats in the United States Football League. His teammates gave him the nickname "Gizmo" from a character in the movie *Gremlins*.

Late in the 1986 season, he signed with the Eskimos, and, before the year ended, Williams unveiled his trademark flip in the end zone after scoring a touchdown on a 74-yard punt return. The Edmonton coaching staff knew they had found a special player, but they weren't sure how to use him.

"When I first came into the league to play my position, there wasn't a position for that," Williams explained. "You had to be a starting receiver or a starting defensive back. And in my first two years, I was so dominant, they decided to make it that you could bring in a punt returner and make it a regular position to play."

In 1987, Gizmo received the first of seven CFL all-star selections. He scored the first missed field-goal return touchdown in regular-season history and then followed it up with what in 2005 was voted the greatest Grey Cup play of all time. In Edmonton's 38–36 victory over Toronto, Williams took Argos kicker Lance Chomyc's missed field goal five yards deep in his own end zone, raced to his right and shifted into overdrive around the corner and down the sideline. Just as defenders were about to stop him at midfield, Gizmo slanted in a long diagonal to the opposite side of the field, sprinting past Chomyc, the last man back. He ran, in total, 115 yards for the touchdown. This was the first and only time in the classic that a missed field goal has been run back to score.

Every CFL team began looking for a player like Gizmo, a game-breaker from a special-teams position. "If a team needed a spark, that was

Gizmo," said former teammate Matt Dunigan. "He'd give it to you."

Williams won two Grey Cups in his remarkable career and retired in 2000 with 17 regular-season and playoff records. After football, Gizmo stayed in the Edmonton area, becoming a personal trainer and giving his time freely to several charities.

He only talks about his tough upbringing with children when discussing drug and alcohol abuse. Gizmo tells everyone the same thing when they ask him about the obstacles he had to overcome: "It makes no difference where you're from or how you start. It's how you finish."

Chapter Eight

The American Influence

The fear of American domination of the Canadian Football League goes back to the early 1900s, when U.S. college football began to grow and develop as a popular and highly viable commercial enterprise. At the same time, Canadian football was stuck with its heritage of British rugby, which did not include the forward pass, a new form of attack that made the American product much more entertaining.

In the 1920s, new rule changes in Canada introduced the forward pass and brought the two brands of football closer together. In 1936, the Winnipeg Blue Bombers began recruiting American players and won a Grey Cup. Four years later, the league instituted an import rule, limiting the number of American players on each roster.

Up until the 1970s, American and Canadian professional football teams paid about the same money, permitting star players from American colleges such as Sam Etcheverry, Ron Lancaster, Joe Kapp, Angelo Mosca and Tom Clements to be lured to Canada by lucrative contracts.

Prior to the 1950s, professional football struggled in the United States. Few NFL teams showed a profit. Several folded or had to be reorganized to survive. It was only in 1966, when the NFL and the upstart AFL merged and the Super Bowl began, that American football became the most popular professional sports league in North America.

Rumours of the NFL coming to Canada gained momentum in the 1970s and 1980s, especially in Montréal and Toronto. In 1972, a group of New York businessmen led by millionaire Robert E. Schmertz bid for a CFL franchise to be located south of the border. Five of the nine teams approved the new team, two votes short of the seven required for expansion to go ahead. The enthusiasm to look at the CFL moving to the U.S. was led by Toronto Argonauts owner John Bassett Sr. At that time, the Argos were leading the CFL in attendance and having to pay the CFL thousands of dollars each season in equalization payments to help the league's poorer teams.

When the SkyDome opened in Toronto in 1989, the Argos' lease agreement did not include exclusivity rights for football. The media jumped on the story, fuelling new rumours that the NFL would be coming to town. Ironically, just a few years later, the CFL, a league on the brink of collapse, looked to America to save the Canadian game.

The Northmen

In 1973, the World Football League was formed to challenge the supremacy of the NFL. A WFL team called the Toronto Northmen was awarded to Johnny F. Bassett, son of Toronto Argonauts owner John Bassett. The team was to commence operations in 1974 and run their operations out of Exhibition Stadium (also owned by the Bassett family), the home of the Argos.

On March 31, 1974, the new league dominated the front page of the sports section in newspapers across Canada and United States when the Northmen signed running backs Larry Csonka and Jim Kiick and receiver Paul Warfield of the Super Bowl–champion Miami Dolphins to a multi-million-dollar, three-year package worth $3.3 million. The three Dolphin stars were to join the new league in 1975 after playing out their options in Miami. Toronto also announced they had signed Leo Cahill (the former Argos coach) as the team's general manager and John McVay, an athletic director at the University of Dayton, to coach.

Across Canada there was immediate concern that the Northmen might destroy the CFL. There was fear that Toronto fans would not be able to support two professional football franchises and that the Argos would not be able to compete against the financial resources available in the new league.

Health minister Marc Lalonde (also the minister responsible for sports) of the ruling Liberal Party warned Bassett to move the team south of the border or they would be legislated out. The Liberal minority government, with the support of the New Democratic Party (NDP), prepared legislation designed to keep the Northmen out of Canada. Lalonde announced that the CFL was a Canadian institution and that other professional football teams from the United States would not be welcome.

At first Bassett was defiant, announcing that the Northmen would legally challenge any legislation that would force them to move. Lalonde responded by introducing a bill that would ban

U.S. football leagues from operating in Canada. Bassett knew he was fighting a losing battle, and a search for a new home began. He announced the team would be called the "Southmen."

The *Toronto Star* had fun with the controversy. An editorial with the headline, "Bassett Has No Kiick Coming," lampooned the battle between Bassett and Lalonde:

> There's Warfield, there's Csonka and Kiick
> One's tricky, one's powerful, one's quick,
> Paul Warfield plucks passes from out of the air,
> Big Csonka leaves tackles in broken despair,
> While Kiick gives them moves like a terrified hare;
> Oh, gee, but the Northmen would look mighty slick,
> With Warfield and Csonka,
> with Warfield and Csonka,
> With Warfield and Csonka and Kiick.
> But even with Warfield, with Csonka and Kiick,
> Lalonde is determined the Northmen won't stick,
> "Warfield's a flanker perhaps without peer,
> Csonka's well worth it, though frightfully dear,
> And Kiick sure can run but he'll run south of here,"
> At which Johnny Bassett is quietly sick,
> With Warfield and Csonka,
> with Warfield and Csonka,
> With Warfield and Csonka and Kiick.

In the end, Bassett signed a five-year stadium agreement in Memphis. Following that, the federal government quietly withdrew its legislation.

The American Experiment

The CFL of the early 1990s was in desperate shape. The Montréal Alouettes had folded in 1986. Ownership in Ottawa was contending with a growing mountain of debt. The BC Lions, Calgary Stampeders and Toronto Argonauts struggled with uncertainty at the ownership level, while their teams struggled on the field.

Commissioner Larry Smith was given the mandate to begin a bold quest in search for much-needed revenue. For the first time, the league would explore the possibility of expanding south. The National Football League had become the most successful sports league in the world. The price for an NFL franchise had jumped to the hundreds of millions, and only the largest of markets, with substantial corporate support, could provide the financial resources needed to operate a team.

The CFL saw an opportunity to move into smaller markets—cities and regions without large stadiums. The expansion fee was only

$2 million, the payroll a fraction of an NFL franchise. In all, the league would earn $14.3 million in expansion fees at a time when it was sorely needed. But, while the economics seemed favourable, there were many challenges. American fans would have to adapt to CFL rules. There would have to be space inside the stadiums to expand the field to meet Canadian football standards. There was no network television deal—the CFL relied on gate revenues, while NFL owners had become rich on the basis of the TV deals they signed with American networks.

Despite these obstacles, a handful of American owners took the plunge and signed up. Over the course of three seasons, between 1993 and 1995, seven American cities joined the CFL.

It was a roller-coaster ride, and the stories off the field were often bigger than what was happening on the gridiron. It marked a brief period of football madness during which the CFL lost its way in trying to sell their game in the oddest of places—Sacramento, Shreveport, San Antonio, Memphis, Las Vegas, Birmingham and Baltimore. It was doomed to failure, but in that brief three-year period, there were plenty of off-the-wall moments, even by the CFL standard of wackiness.

Viva Las Vegas

The biggest home of legalized gambling in the world, Las Vegas, had tried unsuccessfully to land a franchise in any of North America's big-four professional leagues (Major League Baseball, NFL, NBA or NHL). The big leagues wanted to avoid the connotation of gambling that the city would bring to their sports. Instead, Las Vegas has been home to a series of minor pro teams.

In 1993, the Las Vegas Posse was awarded the second American-based franchise in the CFL. Nick Mileti and his partners paid $3 million to the cash-starved league, and from the start the press revelled in poking fun at the expansion team.

Mileti was a former Cleveland sports broker and World Football League investor. In the 1970s, he had done well selling various sports franchises, but promptly lost his fortune during an ill-advised stint in the movie industry. By investing in the Posse, Mileti was returning to his roots in professional sports.

In order to raise capital to buy the team, Mileti had listed the controlling company, Major League Sports Inc., on the NASDAQ exchange. This generated more than $6 million in capital to get the Posse going.

Before the nickname was finalized, *Maclean's* magazine ran a tongue-in-cheek column suggesting the team be called the "One-Armed Bandits" or the "Rootin' Tootin' Newtons," after perennial Vegas crooner Wayne Newton. The magazine also advised the franchise to play their summer games after midnight to beat the desert heat, redeem ticket stubs for betting chips, hire Vegas showgirls and -guys to sell confections, book the popular Vegas revue "Nudes on Ice" to perform the halftime show and hire Don Rickles as the offensive-line coach.

Like many a tourist's bankroll, the Posse ended up disappearing almost as quickly as they were put together. The team lasted barely half a season in 1994, averaging fewer than 12,000 fans per game in the 32,000-seat Sam Boyd Stadium. When only 5000 people showed up at both their last two home contests, the team moved to Edmonton for one game before dissolving. By that time, Mileti and company had lost an additional $2.24 million in operating revenues.

In their four-month existence, the Posse managed to leave a lasting, highly embarrassing impression. Even before the team took the field, Mileti arranged for Melinda, a magician wearing a G-string and a bikini top, to announce the team name at a press conference at the Lady Luck

Casino. Melinda climbed into a make-believe cannon and, after an explosion spewed confetti and streamers on the small gathering, emerged from a nearby box holding a sign that read POSSE.

The Posse's first training camp was held in the back parking lot of the Riviera Hotel and Casino. The Riviera provided $200,000 in promotions and accommodations for the team. In exchange, the Posse held their training camp on a make-shift practice field that was 70 yards long— 40 yards shorter than CFL regulation, taking the long pass out of the Posse arsenal. Twelve hundred tons of sand topped with grass sod were used to complete the field.

The first Las Vegas exhibition game was held on June 29 in 47° C heat (the temperature on the artificial playing surface). All the seats were aluminum bleachers, testing the resilience of anyone who ventured to sit on them. A reporter from the *Las Vegas Review-Journal* questioned the wisdom of bringing the CFL to the desert: "A crowd of 6280 heat-drained but enthusiastic fans showed up to watch a foreign brand of football in a town full of goofy sports teams."

Mileti was not fazed that the exhibition game was being held during southern Nevada's all-time hottest stretch of weather. He called together reporters and presented a group of cheerleaders sitting on ice blocks while nose tackle Roy Hart took a sledgehammer to a pair of thermometers. Mileti's cheerleaders were among the sport's more scantily clad. During their regular season home opener on July 16, they ran through the Saskatchewan Roughriders' bench area. Roughrider coach Ray Jauch was not impressed, "Naturally the players are going to look at the young ladies and take their minds off the game for at least a few seconds."

The Posse spent hundreds of thousands of dollars marketing that first game, yet the announced crowd was only 12,213 fans. The game was televised across Canada, and a lounge singer named Dennis K.C. Park was hired to sing the national anthem. Park delivered a mangled version of "O Canada" that came out sounding like "O Christmas Tree." The Posse received over 100 complaints, and both Mileti and Park apologized for what had become an international incident. The Posse owner later sent a letter of apology to Prime Minister Jean Chrétien, claiming that his singer (Park was a last minute replacement) was distracted by the stadium's poor sound system. Park subsequently became a sought-after guest on talk shows, and the Tiger-Cats invited him to Hamilton to sing the anthem correctly (which he did).

The Posse decided on a group of riders on horses as the team's mascot. Not unexpectedly, the horses left souvenirs all over the field during pregame festivities. *Sports Illustrated* writer Jack McCallum checked out the Posse and commented, "To say that the team is not drawing flies, therefore, is not entirely accurate. In fact, the Posse pooper-scooper crew has become a fan favourite. The team has not."

Before folding, the team had shaved its ticket prices to $9, and the price of Major League Sports, Inc. shares had dropped from $6.00 to $1.25. At the team's next-to-last home game against the Blue Bombers, only 2350 fans showed up—and about half of the crowd had made the trip from Winnipeg.

The Shreveport Pirates

The Shreveport Pirates joined the CFL in 1994. The team's first training camp was scheduled for Louisiana State University, but a scheduling foul-up meant that the Pirates had to use the state fair grounds, which at the same time was hosting a circus.

The animals were housed on the main floor. The players were put on the second level—

between 12 and 18 players were forced to share one large, barracks-style room, which included only a single bathroom. Pirates' defensive end Johnny Scott described the bizarre routine when the players headed to practice: "The monkeys tried spitting on us, and the tigers would try pissing on you. It was stinky, too."

The smell was overpowering in the Louisiana heat, though the air conditioning helped a little bit. One of the players, Joe Mero, took one look at the facilities and booked a nearby motel at his own expense.

To make matters worse, the Pirates' first coach was John Huard, who had never coached at the professional level. Huard had been a college coach at the Division III Maine Maritime Academy and brought a drill sergeant mentality to the job. During training camp, he openly berated a volunteer athletic therapist on loan from a nearby hospital. The players watched as the therapist threw his equipment into his truck, never to return. The hospital had provided the therapist in their role as a sponsor of the team. A few days later, Huard was fired without even having the chance to coach in a league game.

"It was not a good way to start the season," said Gregg Stumon, one of the veteran players who had survived Huard's training camp. In fact, the team was completely disorganized. Both the general manager and the team owners (the Gliebermans, Bernie and Lonie) had brought players to camp without talking to one another. Some of the players had been out of professional football for several years.

The new coach, Forrest Gregg, an NFL Hall of Fame tackle, looked at the talent level of the bunch and began to make more roster moves. Within a few days, he had talked the Gliebermans into firing both the team's vice president of operations and the general manager so he could get on with the job of remaking the Pirates.

Sportswriter Kent Heitholt of the *Shreveport Times* summed up the first season of the Pirates: "The team suffered through the quickest firing of a head coach in history, the longest consecutive starting losing streak in history (0–14) and more rain-plagued games than the Amazon basin."

The Pirates were a better team in 1995, winning four of their first 13 games. In July, Steve Davis of the *Dallas Morning News* made the trip to Shreveport to see his first CFL game. He commented, "You hear 'O Canada' spitting from the outdated PA system, and it's the first clue that you're in for an odd night. Pretty soon, you'll realize what's wrong here. It feels like it's 130 degrees. It's not exactly football weather, and yet they are about to play football, Canadian-league style."

As the Pirates continued to struggle on the field, attendance dropped from 12,000 per game in 1994 to 8000 a year later. The team had only 5000 season-ticket holders. The Pirates announced that they needed to boost this number to 15,000 by the start of the 1996 season. Instead, only 2000 fans renewed their season tickets. Finally, after losing $3.5 million, the Gliebermans announced that they were looking to relocate the franchise. A proposed move to Norfolk, Virginia, never materialized, and the Pirates quietly faded away.

The Baltimore No-Names

The CFL was in the right place at the right time when Virginia sports-restaurant owner Jim Speros put down a deposit for a franchise in Baltimore, Maryland, on June 11, 1993. Nine years earlier, the NFL had left town when Colts' owner Robert Irsay had moved the team to Indianapolis in the dead of night.

The Colts' move was a stunning blow to the fans of Baltimore, who had been among the most passionate in the league. When the city failed to get an expansion NFL franchise in 1993, Speros decided it was time to take advantage of the anti-NFL backlash by introducing Canadian football to Baltimore.

As the team president, Speros decided to try to avoid the mistakes the other American CFL teams had made. He lured Don Matthews away from Saskatchewan to become the head coach and told him to build the team as if it were based in Canada. Baltimore signed Tracy Ham, a proven CFL pivot, to be the first quarterback. The team then signed several CFL free agents and even offered contracts to several Canadian players (only one took them up on the offer).

The city of Baltimore agreed to pay for upgrades to aging Memorial Stadium and the club received a $1-a-year lease. Speros also made deals with several local businesses in exchange for season's tickets. Just as the team was gaining momentum, however, an American court ruled that the football team could not be called the Baltimore Colts, as that would constitute trademark infringement. So, for their first season in 1994, the team officially remained nameless (though the team used a logo depicting a horse). For lack of anything better, during that year they were referred to as the "Baltimore Football Club" or the "Baltimore CFLers."

On the field and in the stands, the expansion team was easily the most successful of the American franchises. The club brought in a reported $8.5 million in revenue (enough to break even), averaged 36,499 fans per game and made the playoffs with a 12–6 record. The team defeated Winnipeg and Toronto in the playoffs to advance to the Grey Cup against the BC Lions in Vancouver. It took a Lui Passaglia field goal late in the fourth quarter for the Lions to defeat the no-namers 26–23.

The game had been promoted as a Canada-vs.-U.S. battle. *Vancouver Sun* reporter Pete McMartin did his best to whip up some nationalistic feelings: "This is not the first time a Baltimore team has met a Canadian team in a championship. They met once before. It was for the championship of North America in a series known as the War of 1812. The best Baltimore managed even with the home-field advantage was a draw. Baltimore played a defensive game. We were on offence."

Baltimore adopted the slogan "Unfinished Business" and vowed to win the Grey Cup in 1995. In the off-season, Speros decided on a name, the "Stallions," partly because the team's logo would not have to be changed.

The Stallions were once again a league power-house, but attendance dropped in the team's second year. The CFL as a novelty had begun to wear off—Baltimore had signed up only 9000 season-ticket holders, and the team was on track to lose $1.5 million. Then, on November 4, 1995, the day before the CFL playoffs were to begin, sources leaked that Art Modell, owner of the NFL Cleveland Browns was moving his team to Baltimore in 1996.

It was the worst possible news for the Stallions. The story grabbed media attention away from the team, and Baltimore football fans were once again riveted to the NFL. The Browns had a long and proud history, but the municipal government in Cleveland had ignored Modell's requests to upgrade the 80,000-seat Cleveland Memorial Stadium.

Baltimore offered a rich incentive deal to move the Browns. Money the Stallions had counted on from corporate sponsors began drying up in anticipation of the NFL's return. A vocal group of Stallions fans, however, showed up for Baltimore's first playoff game against San Antonio. They declared their affection for the CFL and voiced their displeasure in the expensive ticket prices demanded in the NFL.

The Stallions defeated San Antonio, advancing to the Grey Cup to face the Calgary Stampeders with Doug Flutie. This time Baltimore handily defeated their Canadian opponent 37–20 before over 52,000 fans at Taylor Field in Regina. For the first time, Lord Grey's trophy was heading south of the border.

Baltimore Sun sports columnist Ken Rosenthal wrote: "A country that already suffers from an inferiority complex is going to require nation-wide psychiatric assistance now that a U.S. team—a potentially homeless U.S. team—has won the Grey Cup for the first time."

In Baltimore, only 200 fans showed up for a downtown rally to celebrate the championship. Not one Baltimore television station had sent a crew to Regina to cover the game. With the NFL's impending return to Baltimore, it seemed that the city had moved on—the CFL was considered a second-rate league, the Stallions a B-level team.

In late November, Speros announced a "Save Our Stallions" campaign, setting a January 5 deadline to sell 20,000 season tickets. The team was $800,000 in debt, had lost significant sponsorship dollars and turfed almost all their office staff. In the meantime, Speros began looking at moving the team to another city. Several

American sites were considered, but by January it seemed that Montréal had become the front-runner.

On January 31, Speros brought the Grey Cup to Montréal to show it off to the media. The move almost backfired when newspapers ran a photo showing the trophy being carted around in a green garbage bag. A few days later the league officially announced that, after an almost 10-year absence, the Montréal Alouettes were back in the CFL. At the same time, the CFL's board of governors also declared the American experiment was over—the CFL was back to nine Canada-based franchises.

In their short history, the Stallions had played in two Grey Cup games and taken home the winning trophy in only their second year of existence. The team had averaged over 25,000 fans in that period—the CFL expansion gamble had been a dismal failure, except in Baltimore where football fans showed up in large numbers to watch the Canadian game.

Chapter Nine

A Plug for the CFL—Selling Canadian Football

In a manner similar to Canada's insecurity about its place in the world (especially compared to its neighbour to the south), CFL football has struggled to find a comfortable niche in the sporting world. Invariably the league is unfairly compared to the NFL, and, predictably it seems, the CFL responds to take the bait.

In 1996, the league ran an ad campaign with the banner "Radically Canadian." The goal was to take a new marketing approach and aggressively promote a product that at the time was struggling to find an identity. In advertising, however, there is a fine line between what is perceived as "edgy" versus just plain offensive.

The campaign started with a new slogan—Our Balls Are Bigger—that was meant to create a more macho image for the league, especially in comparison to the NFL. Not surprisingly, the slogan was met with a mixed reaction upon its release.

Vicki Hall of the *Edmonton Journal* wrote: "What a fitting marketing slogan—for a male escort agency." Winnipeg general manager Cal Murphy publicly stated that the campaign was in poor taste. Edmonton boss Hugh Campbell regretted that his team didn't "scream bloody murder as loud as we should have."

There was also criticism that the slogan was somewhat inaccurate. Players interpreted the slogan to mean that the CFL football was bigger than the NFL's. A decade earlier that was true, but in the 1990s the dimensions of both footballs were nearly identical.

"There's no difference in the balls now," said Winnipeg quarterback Kent Austin after the slogan was unveiled. "I used to have a tough time holding CFL footballs because they were so big. But they're the same size as the NFL balls these days."

Jeff Giles, the CFL's chief operating officer, defended the new approach. "We wanted something with an edge to it," said Giles. "We want our fans to stand up with passion and courage and say, 'I'm Canadian and proud of it.'"

The testosterone-flavoured campaign continued that summer with the launch of T-shirts with One Tough Mother emblazoned on the front. Giles said the slogan reflected the league's new attitude: "We take pride in our toughness and resiliency and our Canadian identity and the fact we're not changing our game for anybody."

"Our objective already has been met because people are talking about us—negatively or positively," explained the CFL executive.

Many die-hard Canadian football supporters wondered if the league was spinning too hard a message in an attempt to sell its product. They may have had a point; the CFL has a lengthy legacy of rabid fans that have kept the Canadian football tradition alive and, if not well at all times, at least hanging in there.

A Perfect Season for Calgary's Fantastic Fans

It took the Calgary Stampeders 37 years to put together a team good enough to represent the West in the Grey Cup classic, so, when the team and many of its fans made the trip to Toronto for the 1948 game against Ottawa, there was already much to celebrate. Until this time, the Grey Cup was anything but a festive happening. It was not yet a celebration of a Canadian sporting tradition—the event was mostly about football, mostly about an Eastern team romping over the Western representative, and mostly the game was held in Toronto.

The 1948 Calgary Stampeders were a special team. After losing to Winnipeg a year earlier in the Western final, the Stamps were determined to improve. To accomplish this, player-coach Les Lear, who had become the first Canada-trained player to star in the NFL, was lured to Calgary after five seasons south of the border.

The all-star lineman had played five seasons in Winnipeg between 1938 and 1942, winning two Grey Cups. For four straight seasons, he was voted to *MacLean's* magazine's all-Canadian team. Lear was born in the United States but learned football in Winnipeg, playing with the Deer Lodge Juniors and later for the University of Manitoba.

With Lear on board, the Stampeders won all 12 league games to become the first and only undefeated team in CFL history. Football fans in Calgary were thrilled to have finally advanced to the Grey Cup game, and a large contingent decided to cheer the team on in Toronto.

Upon arriving in Canada's biggest city, the Calgarians decided that the Grey Cup should be about more than football; most of all, it should be about having a good time. As hosts of the Stampede, promoted as the greatest outdoor show on earth, the Wild Westerners decided to bring their party east. Calgary alderman Don MacKay was among the first to recognize that the event needed an injection of jollity. It started with the Grey Cup Special, a train that carried the team and its supporters on a whistle-stop trip through Medicine Hat, Moose Jaw, Brandon, Barrie and dozens of other towns all the way to Toronto. Once in the big city, the visitors used the week leading up to the game to invent the Grey Cup Festival.

Out came the white Stetsons and the horses to go with them. The normally regal Royal York Hotel was taken over by hundreds of Calgary fans, chuckwagons and all. Hotel management wisely cleared out the furniture in the lobby when the visitors began riding their steeds inside. For three nights, there was singing in the streets of downtown Toronto and the sounds of horses' hooves echoing among the buildings. On the steps of Toronto City Hall, the Westerners hosted the first pancake breakfast, now a tradition during Grey Cup week. In short, the old town had been woken up.

The Calgarians' enthusiasm was rewarded when the Stampeders upset the highly favoured Rough Riders 12–7. Best of all, the Calgary fans had left a legacy—the annual celebrations surrounding Canada's football championships grew into a week-long event. A Miss Grey Cup beauty pageant was started, and the Grey Cup parade became a fixture. Millions of Canadians threw Grey Cup parties for their friends and families, as television brought the game to the rest of the country.

All of the hoopla that now is the Grey Cup was started almost 60 years ago—and none of it was scripted. Legendary running back Normie Kwong was just a rookie back then, but remembers the origin of the Grey Cup Festival:

> It was a really spontaneous time. Everything happened just because someone thought of it at the time. Nothing was planned. On the way back, people met us at every little whistle stop along the way, and the coach made sure that one or two players were always there to greet the people no matter what time of night. There were people there right across Canada.

As the Calgary players and fans celebrated the victory after the game ended, Les Lear made an appearance later that evening at the Toronto Men's Press Club with the Grey Cup tucked under one arm. Milt Dunnell, the *Toronto Star*'s legendary columnist, said Lear showed up to "rub it in to the Eastern scribes and celebrate with the Westerners and Western ex-pats like Jim Coleman [another Canadian sports-writing legend]." Dunnell said he was "like the vast majority of people here in not giving the Grey Cup a second thought until the Calgarians descended on a sleepy city, determined to outlaw fun, and turn it into the huge event it was for decades after."

Mayhem in Vancouver

The BC Lions entered the league in 1954, the last of the original nine teams to join the CFL. The Lions had the most modern facility in Canadian football, the 25,000 seat Empire Stadium, built to host the 1954 British Empire and Commonwealth Games. The only problem was that the Leos stank for their first five seasons, not getting a whiff of a playoff spot until 1959, when they made the post-season with a 9–7 record.

BC was selected to host the Grey Cup game in 1960, but unfortunately the Lions slipped to 5–9–2 and missed the playoffs once again. For that reason, perhaps, Vancouver fans were in an ugly mood even before the big game between

Ottawa and Edmonton began. And it only got worse. With the Rough Riders comfortably ahead 16–6 in the final minute, a mob ran onto the field and began trying to pull down the goalposts. The referees huddled with the players to decide on a course of action.

Meanwhile, the crowd on the field grew to about 5000. The 75 policemen, who had been kept busy throughout the contest kicking out drunks and breaking up fights, were powerless to intervene. A teenager raced onto the field, took the football and ran towards the Ottawa end zone, vanishing into the crowd. The PA announcer's pleas for the fans to leave the field were ignored, and the referee was ordered by the commissioner to end the game with 41 seconds remaining. The players rushed off the field to the safety of their dressing rooms.

The president of the Eskimos called the whole affair "the most disgraceful exhibition I've ever seen." The CFL considered boycotting Vancouver in the future, but the game had been a box office hit, with over 35,000 paying customers. Economics overruled any possible punishment, and the Grey Cup once again came to the West Coast in 1963 and 1966.

Each return created more controversy. In 1963, the Lions were a league power, led by the offensive duo of quarterback Joe Kapp and running back Willie Fleming. BC would be hosting the Grey Cup on their home turf, and over 36,000 fans stuffed into the stadium to see the Lions take on the Hamilton Tiger-Cats.

The Tiger-Cats had a tough defence anchored by Angelo Mosca, a scowling 268-pound tackle with a reputation as a headhunter. In the second quarter, Mosca riled up the fans when he jumped on Fleming with a borderline hit on the sidelines after the slim runner had already been taken down. The collision knocked Fleming out of the game with a concussion. Kapp was incensed that a penalty was not called on the play, and the Vancouver fans vocally agreed with their quarterback. Perhaps surprisingly, a riot did not ensue even though Hamilton went on to a convincing 21–10 victory.

Three years later, the relative docility of the West-Coast audience again disappeared. Like the 1960 contest six years earlier, spectators again raced onto the field with four seconds remaining in Saskatchewan's 29–14 victory over Ottawa. And that was just an unruly warm-up for the main event, the Grey Cup Parade. Officials had decided to depart from tradition by holding the parade after the game rather than the morning before. More than 5000 fans flocked downtown to watch the procession of floats, but after the street festival ended, the hoodlums took over. Rioters broke store windows in the downtown area, ripped apart street decorations, lit fires in trashcans and threw beer bottles at the police. In four hours of disorder, over 700 people were arrested. It took the police nearly 60 hours to process all the charges. In the end, more than 300 people needed lawyers.

The Vancouver newspapers devoted pages to the riot, and civic authorities said the lawlessness was led by a criminal element intent on using the celebration to cause disorder. Vancouver city prosecutor Stewart McMorran cited a case where a man had given his girlfriend bail money before he headed downtown for the parade.

The Not-So-Big Payout

In 2005, the Wendy's restaurant chain sponsored the CFL's first "Kick-for-a-Million" contest. A fan was randomly selected from nearly 200,000 online entries to travel to Toronto for an October game between the Argos and the Hamilton Tiger-Cats. At halftime, the winner was given the opportunity to attempt four field goals from different distances for a variety of prizes. The nationally televised event culminated in a 50-yard attempt worth a million dollars.

The kickoff contest was modelled after a similar promotion in the NHL in which a fan in Washington won $1 million for shooting a puck the length of the ice and through a small opening in a board placed in front of a hockey net. In the CFL version, Brian Diesbourg would get four kicks from varying distances—the longer the field goal, the bigger the prize. Things didn't look good for the Belle River, Ontario, native as he missed a 20-yard try for $1000 cash, a 30-yarder for a digital imaging package and a 40-yard attempt for a home theatre package.

Each of the kicks had plenty of distance but just sailed wide of the uprights. After anxiously waiting out a five-minute commercial break on TSN, the 25-year-old mechanical engineer lined up the 50-yard try in front of just over 40,000 spectators at Rogers Centre. Diesbourg nailed the long kick through the uprights (no small accomplishment, since professional placekickers convert less than 50 percent of their long field-goal attempts in game situations).

"It's unbelievable," said Diesbourg, a long-time soccer player who had never kicked a football before the event. "When it left my foot, I was hoping it went left because I just missed the first three to the right. I purposely kicked it to the left hoping it would even itself out and it did. I knew I hit it good, but I wasn't sure if it was good enough because I kind of lost the ball before it went through. But then I looked and the official raised his hand to signal it was good, and then I knew for sure. It was surreal."

After making the kick, the stadium erupted in cheers, and members of the Argos mobbed Diesbourg before returning to the field for the second half. Toronto kicker Noel Prefontaine was one of the first players to congratulate the contest winner. Diesbourg had been allowed one workout with Prefontaine a day earlier. At the practice session, he had showed a strong leg in making five out of eight attempts from 40 yards. Even though he missed all five from 50 yards out, he had plenty of distance.

"Having had the opportunity to work with him, he did show the leg strength," said Prefontaine after the winning kick. "I think his soccer background really helped him. I thought he had a legitimate shot."

What should have been feel-good story became a national controversy when it was announced that the million dollars was actually a $25,000-per-year annuity paid over 40 years. Wendy's was slammed by media across the country. The resulting furor resulted in Wendy's changing the payout, and Diesbourg became an instant millionaire. The Kick-for-a-Million contest has since become an annual event on the CFL schedule.

The Tripper

The Hamilton Tiger-Cats mauled the Winnipeg Blue Bombers 32–7 in the 1957 Grey Cup game— a contest that featured one of the oddest unrehearsed plays in the history of the classic. Late in the fourth quarter, with Hamilton ahead 25–0, Ray "Bibbles" Bawel, a Tiger-Cat defensive back, intercepted a Blue Bomber pass and began running untouched down the sideline, on his way for sure touchdown.

In those days, "field seats" were set up next to the playing field, and as Bawel made his way towards the end zone, a fan suddenly stuck out his leg, sending Bawel face-first into the turf at the Winnipeg 42-yard line. The stadium hushed, expecting a rumble and perhaps an arrest—the tripper was actually sitting next to a police officer. Bawel did rush to his feet and race over to the fan, but no fisticuffs ensued, just a good old-fashioned tongue-lashing from several of the Hamilton players.

The mysterious spectator dressed in a trench coat and a black Ivy League-style cap soon faded into the crowd and left the stadium. A reporter thought he recognized the tripper as a Winnipeg bookmaker, which led to some wild speculation about a gambling racket. Further investigation put reporters on the trail of a prominent Toronto lawyer.

The tripper turned out to be David Humphrey, later Mr. Justice Humphrey of the Ontario Court (General Division). Thirty-five years after the incident, Humphrey described why he had sent the Hamilton player tumbling. During the course of the game, the lawyer had encountered a man on the sideline who had been a jury foreman in a criminal proceeding in which Humphrey had represented the accused. The lawyer had lost the case; the accused was convicted and sentenced to death. Humphrey blamed the jury foreman for the unfavourable verdict. When Humphrey saw the man, he simply blew a gasket and, fuelled by a dose of temporary insanity, ended up tripping the unlucky Tiger-Cat as he sped down the sideline.

The blatant case of fan interference didn't change the outcome of the game. Bawel was named outstanding player—besides the interception, he had returned a fumble for a touchdown and knocked down several other passes. Incredibly, only two months earlier, the Hamilton defender had been released by the Philadelphia Eagles and was set to retire.

Months after the game, a package was received at Bawel's home in Evansville, Indiana. Inside a box was a $150 gold watch. Inscribed on the back was, "From the Tripper, Grey Cup 1957." There were no hard feelings after the incident, and years later, the two still kept in touch.

The Cost of Cheering Up a Province

CFL fans living in one of the league's big cities—Toronto, Montréal or Vancouver—may not understand how important the Roughriders are to the people of Saskatchewan. The Riders are the province's team. A plaque dedicated at the club's silver anniversary in 1977 has on it the names of 304 cities, towns, villages and hamlets that have supported the Green Machine. Taylor Field may stand in Regina, but fans who make the trip from places like Biggar, Oxbow, Eyebrow and Cut Knife fill the stadium.

There was then a lot riding on the 1989 Grey Cup, one of the best classics ever played. Inside the comfort of Toronto's SkyDome, a record crowd of 54,088 fans watched Saskatchewan edge Hamilton 43–40. Roughriders kicker Dave Ridgeway booted the winning field goal on the second-to-last play of the game. It was a Cinderella finish because Saskatchewan had headed into the playoffs as a third-place team. Two upset victories in Calgary and Edmonton had provided the Roughies a ticket to the big game.

For 10 years, the economy of Saskatchewan had been slammed with low wheat prices, rural depopulation and crop failures. For 23 years, the province had been without a Grey Cup victory. After Ridgeway's winning kick, things went a little crazy.

First, there were the Roughrider fans inside the SkyDome. They carried banners from their communities—whether it was Lancer, Lanigan, Gull Lake or Weyburn—reminding everyone that the Roughriders are truly a provincial team. The seats were filled with fans wearing Rider green. They stayed after the game, and even after their heroes had left the stadium, they were still singing "Green is the Colour."

The Toronto *Globe and Mail* described the scene in Regina: "Within an hour of the game's conclusion, traffic on Regina's main arteries had ground to a standstill as Roughrider fans whooped and waved banners and flags from the backs of their pickup trucks. Albert Street, the city's main north-south thoroughfare, was shut down for several kilometres by ecstatic fans, who soon abandoned their vehicles and wandered through the streets. The drivers of huge semi-trailers joined in the celebration blowing their foghorns."

When the Riders returned home, 18,000 fans showed up at Taylor Field in –10° C weather to welcome the club and cheer for everyone associated with the team from the coaches to the ball boys to the office staff.

Less than three weeks later, a sobering message was delivered to those in attendance at the club's annual meeting. Saskatchewan's long playoff run had almost bankrupted the team. Instead of making an $85,000 profit, the Riders had lost $195,000—the extra cost of playing three post-season games on the road. General Manager Al Ford summed up the irony of the team notching its most exciting championship: "Winning the Grey Cup cost the Saskatchewan Roughriders more than a quarter of a million dollars and pushed the team's debt to an almost unmanageable $1.6 million."

Of course, the team somehow managed to deal with the almost unmanageable debt. After all, this was a team that in the early years used one football for the entire game and then raffled it off. At one point, the Riders were so financially strapped that players going off the field had to strip their jerseys and hand them to the players going on. In the Dust Bowl droughts of the 1930s, many farmers were so short of cash that they traded what was left of their wheat crops for season tickets. The 1989 Grey Cup victory wasn't enough to do the Riders in; the Green Machine hums on with a whole province still watching and supporting their team.

Pamela Anderson—Discovered by the CFL

Three weeks before new Lions owner Murray Pezim took his team on a wacky two-year journey, a star was discovered in the stands of BC Place Stadium. During a July 1989 game against the Toronto Argonauts, a cameraman was panning the crowd, looking for a fan to show on the stadium's big screen.

Not surprisingly, the camera stopped on a busty, striking blonde wearing a Labatt T-shirt.

The exuberant fan was jumping up and down while the crowd did "the Wave." When she sat down, the fans kept cheering until she stood up again to acknowledge the applause. Even the players were distracted by all the noise. At half-time she was brought down to field level, where she drew the winning ticket for the 50–50 draw.

The Labatt people in attendance took note and quickly hired the young woman to take part in an ad campaign, which led to a nude layout in *Playboy* magazine. She later starred in the TV series, *Baywatch*, playing a lifeguard named C.J. Parker, a role that required her to wear a swimsuit for most of every episode. Thanks to lots of hair bleach—she is a natural brunette—and breast augmentation, Pamela Anderson became the symbol of Californian babe-dom.

Over the years, Anderson has become a staple of the tabloid media—a career based more on celebrity than talent. And all because of a chance appearance on a Jumbotron at a CFL game.

Krazy George—Professional Cheerleader

He is balding, long-haired and scruffily dressed. For 28 years he has jumped around, banged his

drum and organized cheers. And in that time he has bothered lots of people, especially opposing players and coaches.

Krazy George Henderson, the energetic, tom-tom-thumping cheerleader is now 63 years old. His website says he has appeared before 25 million fans and has been seen by hundreds of millions more on television. He claims to be the first professional cheerleader.

Krazy George refined his routine as a fan in the stands in 1968 at San Jose State University. For the next seven years, he became famous in the San Francisco Bay area, attending various college and minor professional games. In 1975, the owner of the Kansas City Chiefs brought him in for one home game. His act went over so well that for the next five years, he became a regular at Chiefs games. A career was born.

In 1981, Henderson became famous for introducing "the Wave" during an Oakland Athletics playoff baseball game against the New York Yankees. It took him three years to perfect the move, in which fans take turns, by section, standing up and waving their arms. He had tried the cheer a couple of times at high school rallies, then mastered a simpler version at San Jose State where just three sections of the stadium took part.

Over 20 professional teams have used Henderson's services regularly over the last quarter century. The BC Lions were one of his most consistent employers—Krazy George worked Lions games for 11 years. When the team moved to BC Place Stadium in 1983, Henderson was a perfect fit. The new facility was a hit, and over 50,000 fans regularly attended Lions games. The stadium was Canada's first domed facility, a perfect venue for Krazy George to amplify an already noisy challenge for visiting teams. He quickly built a reputation as the Leos' secret weapon.

Krazy George has a special charisma that fires crowds up. He stage-manages fans into doing what he wants by utilizing a tool kit of tricks—self-effacing humour, wild-man threats, banging on his drum and, of course, orchestrating the Wave. In a time when fads quickly fade, it seems that the Wave has stood the test of time.

"As a professional cheerleader, I know why I do it. What it does is intensify the energy of the crowd," explained Henderson to an *American Press* sportswriter. "It's almost like an accomplishment. It's their own competition, like a contest or video game. You have to participate to make it work. It takes 95 percent of fans doing it to make it great."

"You can start a Wave, but nobody can stop one. The only way it stops is if something exciting happens on the field."

On the eve of the 1994 Grey Cup game at BC Place, the hometown Lions and the Baltimore CFLers made a backroom deal. The Lions agreed to put a muzzle on the Fan-O-Meter, a scoreboard gadget that displays the level of crowd noise in an attempt to motivate spectators to cheer louder. In return, the Leos were allowed to let Krazy George loose. "We won that battle," said BC General Manager Eric Tillman. "Baltimore felt that this should be a neutral site."

Henderson played up the fact that he had become a point of discussion. "What? They had a meeting about me? I think it's fantastic; I love it. I will do cheers, but it will probably turn into straight noise."

The most winning CFL coach of all-time, Don Matthews, was in charge of the Baltimore team. His staff countered the expected bedlam by providing earplugs, wristbands with play instructions on them, body signals and silent counts.

"Crowd noise is a real, maybe deciding factor if you don't prepare for it," said Matthews. "This time, we'll be ready."

In the end, Krazy George wasn't needed to encourage the fans in the Grey Cup game in Vancouver. He started his trademark Wave, but there was a constant din inside the stadium as BC and Baltimore battled each other to the final whistle. In the end, 55,000 fans were on their feet as Lions kicker Lui Passaglia kicked a 29-yard field goal with 1:25 remaining to defeat Baltimore 26–23.

Open for Business

September 11, 2001—a date inscribed in the collective consciousness of North Americans; a date when chaos and uncertainty briefly ruled when a small terrorist organization called Al Qaeda attacked the United States, bringing down four passenger jets, destroying the Twin Towers of the World Trade Center in New York City and killing over 2000 people.

Following the terrorist attacks, every sports organization in North America—the NFL, MLB, NCAA, PGA and NASCAR—announced that they would postpone their games or events at least through the following weekend. Every sports organization, that is, except the CFL.

It was a highly charged decision. Half of the league's general managers, coaches and players were American, as well as two of the owners. The league wanted to appear sympathetic, but in a gate-revenue-driven business, cancelling games would have created financial hardship.

On September 14, CFL Commissioner Michael Lysko announced that the four games scheduled on the weekend would go ahead. Lysko was obviously uncomfortable with the decision, but was bound to follow the direction he had been given by the league board of governors. David Asper, a CFL governor and Winnipeg Blue Bombers owner, was actually rumoured to have pushed the idea of playing the games, stating that league would have the sports world to itself. The player representatives from all the CFL teams also supported the decision.

A day later, Commissioner Lysko said he was in favour of postponing the games, but no official league decision had been made. The two American owners, Montréal's Robert Wetenhall and Toronto's Sherwood Schwarz, were reported to have reconsidered. The players were also worried about the decision, and sports talk-radio stations and other media were letting the CFL know that they had made a foolish decision.

As public scrutiny intensified, the eight teams playing on the weekend began trying to get to their destinations. Air travel had been badly disrupted by the attacks. The Tiger-Cats, who were scheduled to play in Vancouver, and the Eskimos, who were to play in Winnipeg, had wisely trucked their equipment ahead of time. The Roughriders made it to Calgary, only to find out their game against the Stampeders would be pushed ahead a day because the federal government had announced that a national day of mourning was to be held on game day. Hamilton's flight to Vancouver was cancelled just a few hours before it was due to leave—it would be a long shot for the team to find another flight in time.

Edmonton players arrived at the airport to find their flight to Winnipeg had also been cancelled. Another plane was available later the same morning, but it developed mechanical problems and could not take off. Eskimos president Hugh Campbell sent his team home and, without league sanction, the game was cancelled.

Commissioner Lysko was put in a no-win situation. The media and most fans wanted the games rescheduled, but his employers insisted the games be played. Fortunately for Lysko, the turmoil in the air industry allowed him to call off all four games. Winnipeg was not happy with Lysko's decision, despite the bad publicity the league had already received. Blue Bombers owner Asper and coach Dave Ritchie accused the Eskimos of shying away from playing their team in Winnipeg. They also went after Lysko for allowing Edmonton to cancel the game, all the while claiming that they did not want to appear insensitive to the tragedy that had occurred.

And the CFL was not immune to the effects of the terrorist attacks. The best friend of Calgary lineman Joe Fleming's wife was on board one of the airliners that had crashed. Winnipeg linebacker Brian Clark, a graduate of a university in New Jersey, had several classmates who worked in the World Trade Center. The son of Alouettes owner Robert Wetenhall had also worked there, but fortunately had not gone into the office that day. Several other American players had family or friends who worked in or close to New York, Washington or the other crash site in Pennsylvania. It was not the time to play football.

The league was able to reschedule three of the four games for the following Monday. The Hamilton-BC contest went ahead two days after the final regular-season game. Lions owner David Braley criticized Lysko's scheduling decision—it meant his squad had to play three games in eight days, including a playoff match.

In the end, Michael Lysko's tenure as CFL boss became very shaky after the terrorist attacks. Through the crisis, Lysko had shown no reluctance in publicly criticizing the decisions made by the CFL governors. The tension between the commissioner and several of the owners intensified. In March 2002, Lysko was fired—the first CFL boss to lose his job.

The Bachelor

Jesse Palmer had a dream. As a kid growing up in Ottawa, he wanted to be a quarterback—an NFL quarterback, leading his team to victory at the Super Bowl. It was a tall order. No Canadian had been a starting QB in any professional football league since Russ Jackson back in the 1960s. And that was in the CFL.

Palmer certainly had the physical tools. He dominated in high-school football—he could throw the ball deep and accurately. He was strong—his 6'2", 225-pound frame could withstand the rigours of facing defensive linemen. He was durable and mobile.

Major American universities came calling with scholarship offers. He finally decided on the University of Florida Gators, where head coach Steve Spurrier had the reputation of being one of the best teachers in the American college game. And the dream continued when Palmer made the roster of the New York Giants.

And then came the long apprenticeship required of most young quarterbacks in the NFL. Spending hours on the practice field and watching film, holding a clipboard on the sidelines and waiting for an opportunity. In the meantime, the Montréal Alouettes had selected the young prospect 15th overall in the 2001 CFL college draft, optimistic that one day they might get a shot at bringing him back to Canada.

In December 2003, Palmer was given an opportunity when the Giants' starting quarterback was hurt. For three games, he was New York's starting QB—the first Canada-trained quarterback to start an NFL game. He did okay, not enough to earn the spot on a full-time basis, but he showed enough talent and potential to keep the dream alive.

And then, as Palmer settled in once again on the sidelines, an unexpected opportunity came calling. He auditioned for a spot on a new reality series called *The Bachelor*. His good looks and athletic background were a perfect fit for the title role. The show was a hit. Palmer became famous across North America as television audiences watched each week to see which young woman would make the final cut.

In the huge media market of New York, Palmer was offered part-time television football analyst jobs with three local stations. On the football field, however, Palmer stagnated on the Giants' depth chart. He was being well compensated (around $600,000 per season) to be the backup, but his dream of glory in the NFL was rapidly fading. He was finally released by the Giants and found a new home with the San Francisco 49ers. But Palmer never fit in with the long-range plans of the 49ers, who had already drafted two young quarterback prospects. He was released in 2006.

After five seasons in the NFL, Palmer was at a kind of crossroads. The 27-year-old had worked as a football analyst for the Fox network, but still felt he had something to prove on the playing field. Palmer had hoped to return to Canada to spend his pre-retirement years playing in the CFL, and although the National Football League had been a disappointment, Canadian football was still a possibility. Montréal general manager Jim Popp came calling, and, two weeks after his release from San Francisco, the Alouettes signed

Palmer to their practice roster for the remainder of the 2006 season, with the opportunity to compete for a starting job the next year.

"I don't know if I'll play in the NFL again. I certainly haven't closed that door, but my attention is on my career in Canada and having success here," Palmer said after signing in Montréal. "I always dreamed of playing in the NFL, but I also always dreamed of playing in Canada. I knew it would happen at some point. It's like I'm living the second part of my dream."

After a 10-year voyage at the elite level in American football, Popp cautioned fans that Palmer would have to readjust to the CFL game. "The odds of him stepping on the field this year are slim," said Popp. "After 10 years of playing U.S. football, now he's coming back and he's being reacclimated when he's never played pro football in the CFL. This is all new."

Russ Jackson, the best Canadian ever to play quarterback in the CFL, also warned that the expectations placed on Palmer should be tempered with his on-the-job experience: "The first thing is he hasn't been real active in terms of playing time, and everyone knows real action is a lot different than practice," he said. "I also think the whole idea of motion is something he's going to have to get used to. Then there is the extra man and the size of the field."

The Alouettes had also been the best team in the Eastern Conference for the last five years and had gone to the Grey Cup in four of those seasons. But the fans in Montréal were getting a bit restless as starting quarterback Anthony Calvillo struggled for the first time in several years. It was hard for the fans not to get excited about a homegrown Canadian, one who had become an international celebrity, possibly challenging for the number-one job.

And though never stating anything publicly, the Alouettes' front office surely considered the possibility of Palmer taking over as the starting QB. It would have been a marketing dream for the Montréal team—a terrific-looking, articulate and talented Canadian quarterback in his prime would have guaranteed big crowds and increased corporate support.

The only problem with this dream scenario was that Palmer would have to show the Alouettes' coaches that he was ready to beat the future hall-of-famer Calvillo for the job. "Anthony Calvillo is our starting quarterback," reiterated Popp. "He will be our starting quarterback until someone unseats him."

Fans hoping for a competitive training camp in 2007 were disappointed when Palmer announced his retirement from the CFL a few months before the season was set to begin. Opportunities in broadcasting were awaiting the Bachelor, and even an optimistic Palmer knew his chances of unseating Calvillo for the top job were slim.

The football dream for Jesse Palmer ended abruptly—a job in television would have to do.

The Green Machine and Taylor Field

When asked how he felt about Regina's Taylor Field, former BC Lions general manager Herb Capozzi said, "I looked it up in the Yellow Pages—under outdoor insane asylums."

They are known as the "Raunchy Roughies," the "Jolly Green Giants" and the "Green Machine"—Saskatchewan Roughriders supporters are loud, loyal and belligerent. Within the confines of their home stadium, they have intimidated many visiting players over the decades. Up until recent years, the fans were able to sit within a few yards of the players benches—27,732 bodies squeezed into the compact design of the park.

John Robertson, a sportswriter in Regina, recalled how difficult it was to even cheer for another team at Taylor Field. In his column, Robertson related the experience of an unnamed fan who made the mistake of wearing a cowboy hat to a Riders game.

> *I was cheering for the Stamps, and, aside from one guy pouring his coffee down my neck, I survived the first half okay. Then I made the mistake of going to the washroom at halftime. I'm in the cubicle minding my own business, when someone next door shouts, "Yea Roughies."*
>
> *So, I give a "Yea Stamps," and the next thing I know, two guys burst in, grab me by the heels and try to drown me. Then they stand me up and punch me in the mouth. I staggered outside and called the nearest cop. He took one look at my cowboy hat and arrested me for being drunk and disorderly.*

In the 1951 Western championship, a record snowfall was predicted for Regina on the day of the game. The Roughriders couldn't afford a tarpaulin to protect the field. Instead, volunteer truckers hauled tons of straw from an agricultural exhibition at a nearby livestock coliseum to act as a snow screen.

The white stuff never arrived. Instead, a warm spell softened the turf. Players on both teams began retching and gasping as their cleats churned up the field that had been melting beneath the heat of the straw. The most recent event at the agricultural fair had been a pig show, and the straw covering the field was mixed with pig manure, the most pungent of livestock droppings. Neither dry cleaning nor repeated washings could get the stench out of the uniforms. After prevailing in the Western championship, the Regina players needed new uniforms for the Grey Cup in Ottawa.

In 1967, the CFL Players' Association requested that the league order the Roughriders to make improvements to the fencing that ringed the ends of the playing field. Over the years, numerous players had been injured after colliding with the knee-high fence made out of two-by-fours and wire mesh. The fans named the area "Hughie's Haven," after receiver Hugh Campbell, who had the knack of knowing how to avoid the fence while opposing defenders would run headlong into it. During the 1967 season, Hamilton receiver Garney Henley became the fence's most celebrated victim. A newspaper story reported the collision: "Garney Henley had gone after a touchdown pass in the third quarter at Regina. He had launched himself flat out in midair and flown headfirst into a post of that kitty-corner end zone fence, broken the post off, dropped like a rock, spread-eagled on the ground and lay so horrible still. Not a sign or a heave of agonized breath even."

Henley was able to shake off his encounter with the fencing, and after the CFL Players' Association lodged a formal complaint, the barrier was taken down.

In that same year in the Western final in Regina, the Saskatchewan players tested several types of shoes to contend with the slippery field. Ron Atkinson, a 16-year defensive lineman, decided on a pair of $10 Hush Puppies with rubber soles. He taped them to his feet and wore them home after the big game. It wasn't the first time the veteran lineman had chosen unconventional footwear. As a junior player in Saskatoon, he had worn a pair of knee-high rubber boots.

The Roughriders have been around since 1910 and have gone through some lean years from time to time. During the 1960s, a season ticket cost between $14 and $42—a lot of money during the years when the crops were poor. The team, sensitive to the plight of its rural supporters, introduced an easy-payment play, allowing fans to name their own payment terms.

In 1966, the year that Saskatchewan won their first Grey Cup, it cost about $700,000 to run the team. Attendance averaged about 16,000 per game, enough to cover the team's costs. That worked out to be about 130,000 fans over the course of the season, which at the time was more than Regina's total population. It was confirmation that once again the Roughies were and continue to be Saskatchewan's team.

Notes on Sources

Ackles, Bob. *The Water Boy*. Mississauga: John Wiley & Sons Canada, 2007.

Calder, Robert, and Gary Andrews. *Rider Pride: The Story of Canada's Best-Loved Football Team*. Saskatoon: Western Producer Prairie Books, 1984.

Cosentino, Frank. *A Passing Game: A History of the CFL*. Winnipeg: Bain & Cox, 1995.

Dunigan, Matt, and Jim Taylor. *Goin' Deep: The Life and Times of a CFL Quarterback*. Madeira Park, BC: Harbour, 2007.

Goodman, Jeffrey. *Huddling Up: The Inside Story of the Canadian Football League*. Don Mills, Ontario: Fitzhenry & Whiteside, 1982.

Kelly, Graham. *The Grey Cup: A History*. Red Deer: Johnson Gorman, 1999.

O'Brien, Steve. *The Canadian Football League: The Phoenix of Professional Sports Leagues*. Morrisville, NC: Lulu, 2004.

Sullivan, Jack. *The Grey Cup Story, 1909–1955*. Toronto: Beattie, 1955.

Sullivan, Jack. *The Grey Cup Story: The Dramatic History of Football's Most Coveted Award*. Toronto: Pagurian, 1970.

Young, Jim, and Jim Taylor. *Dirty 30*. Toronto: Methuen, 1974.

Web Sources

Canadian Football League (n.d.) http://www.cfl.ca/index.php?module=page&id=22 to =26. (accessed August 15 to November 15, 2008).

Canadian Quarterbacks (n.d.) http://www.ticats.ca/article/canadian_quarterbacks. (accessed October 19, 2008).

Inside the Locker Room. http://insideprofessionalsports.blogspot.com/2006/07/ted-hellard-profile.html. (accessed October 31, 2008).

Johnny Rodgers (n.d.) http://cflapedia.com/Players/r/rodgers_johnny.htm. (accessed October 26, 2008).

Krazy George (n.d.) http://www.krazygeorge.com/indexFS.html. (accessed October 19, 2008).

Les Lear (n.d.) http://www.cfhof.ca/index.php?module=page&id=24&player=Lear,%20Les. (accessed October 26, 2008).

CBC Sports. McLoughlin no longer Stampeders President. www.cbc.ca/sports/story/2003/10/27/stampeders031020.html. (accessed October 31, 2008).

CBC News. Welder didn't fumble chance at Grey Cup. www.cbc.ca/sports/story/2006/11/20/cup-fixed.html. (accessed October 19, 2008).

Information was also used from the following print outlets:
Alberta Venture, American Press, Canadian Business, Canadian Press, CanWest News, Edmonton Journal, Globe and Mail, Guelph Mercury, Hamilton Spectator, Hockey News, Maclean's, Montréal Gazette, National Post, Newsweek, Prince George Citizen, Province, Saturday Night Magazine, Star Phoenix, Sports Illustrated, Toronto Star, United Press International, USA Today, U.S. News & World Report, Vancouver Sun, Washington Post, Western Report, Winnipeg Free Press, World Herald.

Stephen Drake

Stephen Drake was born in Vancouver, but grew up near Merritt, BC, where he faithfully watched the BC Lions telecasts each season. When he moved to the coast, he finally had the opportunity to attend Lions games at Empire Stadium. The thrill of walking on the artificial turf at the end of a game, of seeing Lions legends like Lui Passaglia up close kept him hooked on the CFL. When the Leos moved to BC Place Stadium, football supplanted hockey as the toughest sports ticket in town. These days Stephen is a freelance writer and shares space with his wife and two young children. He is the author of two other non-fiction sports titles for OverTime Books.

OverTime Books

If you enjoyed *Weird Facts About Canadian Football*, **be sure to check out these other great titles from OverTime Books:**

WEIRD FACTS ABOUT GOLF: Strange, Wacky & Hilarious Stories
by Stephen Drake
Most golf historians agree that the game was invented in Scotland more than 500 years ago, but the Chinese claim to have invented a game that involved hitting a ball with a stick towards a target as far back as 943 AD. Nowadays, one can play a round on the ice flows of the Arctic, the plains of Africa and in the war zones of Afghanistan and Iraq. The rich history of the sport has produced a wealth of screwball, outlandish and weird tales.
Softcover • 5.25" X 8.25" • 224 pages • ISBN13 978-1-897277-25-6 • $14.95

CANADIAN HOCKEY TRIVIA: The Facts, Stars & Strange Tales of Canadian Hockey
by J. Alexander Poulton
Hockey is so much a part of Canadian life that the former theme song to *Hockey Night in Canada* was called our unofficial national anthem. Read the fascinating facts from Canada's favourite game such as the almost-forgotten Winnipeg Falcons, who were the first Canadian team to win Olympic gold in 1920 and Dennis O'Brien, who holds the record for most NHL teams played for in a single season.
Softcover • 5.25" X 8.25" • 168 pages • ISBN13 978-1-897277-01-0 • $9.95

WEIRD FACTS ABOUT CURLING: Strange, Wacky, Informative & Hilarious
by Geoffrey Lansdell, with contributions by Carla MacKay
Scottish immigrants brought the game "across the pond" in the 18th century. Since then, the roaring game has amassed its fair share of amusing and interesting stories, facts and anecdotes. Read about curling's on-again, off-again status with the Olympic games, flamboyant characters like "Pizza Paul" Gowsell and much more.
Softcover • 5.25" X 8.25" • 256 pages • ISBN13 978-1-897277-30-0 • $18.95

WEIRD FACTS ABOUT CANADIAN SPORTS: Strange, Wacky & Hilarious
by J. Alexander Poulton
Since the beginning of Canada, our athletes have been involved in some of the weirdest moments in sport. Learn facts that will astound, confuse and make you laugh. Discover lesser-known sports Canadians have been playing for years, from rattlesnake hunts to horse apple hockey, read about Wayne Gretzky's fear of flying and so much more.
Softcover • 5.25" X 8.25" • 224 pages • ISBN13 978-1-897277-32-4 • $14.95

Coming Spring 2009

WEIRD FACTS ABOUT BASEBALL: Strange, Wacky & Hilarious Stories
by J. Alexander Poulton
When people think of baseball, they often picture a sport of grace, class and poetic athleticism, but in reality baseball is equally a game of errors, bloopers and crazy moments. *Weird Facts About Baseball* is a collection of the most ridiculous, funny and wacky moments that have happened in the history of the game. From a pitcher biting his own bum with his false teeth to a catcher falling asleep at the plate during a game, this book has it all! If you appreciate the lighter side of sports then you will certainly love *Weird Facts About Baseball*.
Softcover • 5.25" X 8.25" • 224 pages • ISBN13 978-1-897277-28-7 • $14.95

Lone Pine Publishing is the exclusive distributor for OverTime Books.
If you cannot find these titles at your local bookstore, contact us:
Canada: 1-800-661-9017 USA: 1-800-518-3541